AF255216

Jump!
Exploring Our Spiritual Existence

Jump!
Exploring Our Spiritual Existence

Brent D. Bailey

RESOURCE *Publications* · Eugene, Oregon

JUMP! EXPLORING OUR SPIRITUAL EXISTENCE

Resource Publications
An Imprint of Wipf and Stock Publishers
199 W. 8th Ave., Suite 3
Eugene, OR 97401

www.wipfandstock.com

PAPERBACK ISBN: 978-1-6667-3861-2
HARDCOVER ISBN: 978-1-6667-9953-8
EBOOK ISBN: 978-1-6667-9954-5

01/09/23

Contents

Introduction

ONE WOULD THINK THE easiest part of writing a book would be the introduction, but I have written multiple introductions and none of them seemed appropriate. The challenge of writing this introduction is due to the nature of the book's content and the broad scope of what it covers related to our spiritual existence. The spiritual world is one of the things both religion and our own minds tend to put into a box to make it containable and safe. The truth is that all of our boxes are too small and limit an unlimited God while at the same time ignoring other spiritual forces afoot on this earth. I hope the contents of this book are an adventure for your mind and insightful to your spiritual walk no matter what your belief system is.

When you hear people say they don't believe in coincidences, it means they believe something else is in control of the events that appear to be perfectly placed and timed. I am certain there are random coincidences in our lives, but I also believe God is the "Great Orchestrator" who weaves into our lives not-so-random meetings, events, and even lifelong relationships that direct our paths. As we will discuss in chapter one, God is our Abba (Daddy) who takes care of his children, especially those who are actively seeking a relationship with him.

As you read this book, you should know I prayerfully wrote this, composing a chapter each month. I then brought it to a monthly gathering of Christian brothers to study the contents and gain the wisdom and insights from others because I do not want to misrepresent Scripture nor the God who gives us breath. Each night before these gatherings, I actually felt the need to prayerfully and reflectively review what was written because the content that I had penned was often new to my mind as well. This may sound a little odd, but when it comes to spiritually inspired thoughts they do not ultimately belong to us. Put another way, if the thoughts we receive are put into our minds by the Holy Spirit then they were not our thoughts to begin with. We may transfer these thoughts on, but we are not the originator of them. Also, all thoughts should be balanced against Scripture to verify what is truth. I do believe there will be things within these writings you will find completely or somewhat new to your typical thinking and it is my intent to check these new and intriguing ideas with the truth of Scripture.

Within the chapters, I have written about experiences in my own life that I believe reflect God's activity, some in dramatic ways. God works in our lives far more often than we are aware. Unfortunately, many of us may miss God's activity because we are too caught up in ourselves, or we are too overwhelmed by other factors in life. When this happens, we may simply miss seeing and hearing God's presence.

Though this book has been written with a sequential progression of thought for you to follow, the chapters can also be read independently of one another and then used for personal reflection or group study. However, the first three chapters form a foundation for understanding the chapters that follow, so I encourage you to engage with these first.

Before going forward, let me also point out that I often treat interchangeably the members of the triune, Christian God (the Father, the Son, and the Holy Spirit). I may refer to speaking or praying to God the Father, at other times to Jesus, and at other times I refer to this communication through the Holy Spirit. Chapter 6 expresses more about our interaction with the Trinity, but as far as the book is concerned, they are all equal. Yes, they are all separate persons, yet they are equal, of one mind, and unified in will/purpose. Because the Father, Son, and Spirit are one, they are *all* listening to us; all three know our hearts.

Peace,

Doc B

 ____

CHAPTER 1

Jumping Faith

Introductory Thoughts

Whether you are a devout Christian or simply seeking to learn more about a spiritual existence that goes beyond what your physical eyes can gather, then this first chapter is critical to the level and degree you will experience God's presence in your life. I assume some will write off the concept of this first chapter because they feel they are somehow beyond a childlike posture or belief. However, I believe Jesus makes clear that unless we become like children in how we approach our beliefs and God himself, then we risk truly knowing Jesus on a personal level. I also feel that everything else we cover in this book in regard to experiencing our spiritual existence largely hinges on our ability to surrender many falsely conceived religious and secular ideas that all of us gather as time passes. Our adult minds tend to trap us into things that are not accurate when it comes to our relationship with God, so unless we can become as freely open-hearted as children are, we will likely shut out the truth. It is my hope that you can read this chapter like a child, with an openness that allows you to hear what God might be saying to you right now, and throughout this book. Before reading on, I also encourage you to ask God to speak to and soften your heart as you read and reflect, since it should be our desire to understand God's perspective of reality rather than our own.

Faith of a Child

A gleeful child approaches the edge of a swimming pool and stops with her toes positioned just inches away from the edge. She has never jumped in the pool before, and the deep water looks scary. In front of her, just a few feet away, with his feet planted on the bottom of the pool, is her father. With outstretched arms, he encourages his precious child to jump. Suddenly, with delight in the child's eyes, a look of complete confidence comes over her precious face, and without further hesitation she jumps out over the water and into her father's arms. The child's initial fears were overcome by an unquestionable faith that Daddy will take care of me.

Have you considered that God wants us to be that child? Scripture makes it clear that He wants us to have unshakeable faith in him. He wants us to believe the following verse in the book of Romans:

> *"And we know that in all things God works for the good of those who love him, who have been called according to his purpose." Romans 8:28*

God wants us to know that he can, and will, work all things for good. He does not expect us to believe in "bad luck" where "shit happens." He wants us to believe that even when difficult situations in life occur, he is there to make good come from it. We will rarely see the good that comes out of what appears to be bad if we shut down our expectation of good being revealed. In other words, if we close our eyes out of disbelief, we will rarely be open-minded enough to see what happens from God's perspective. We miss seeing God's presence in things because we are not looking for his activity with a childlike faith. Full faith in God will reveal things we would never see if we shut down our hearts and eyes out of disbelief. Let me be clear that living in a childlike state of belief does not mean we abandon our discernment, thought processes, and good judgement. It does mean that we trust, believe, and hope with much greater emphasis than most of us tend to do. It does mean that we have to step out of our hindered adult minds and live with greater faith. In a sense, we have to jump into his presence.

Faith vs Worry

Consider that many of us exercise a negative form of faith. Interestingly, worry is actually faith perverted into a self-destructive and self-prophesying form of beliefs. Worry is dwelling on negative outcomes, while faith is believing good will prevail. How many times have you heard someone say they were worrying about this or that, and sure enough, just as they believed, it came to pass? Faith puts control in our Father's hands while worry puts outcomes into the hands of people, the world, and potentially into the realm of Satan's influence. Faith believes in positive outcomes, even if you can't see the full conclusion, while worry believes in the negative and removes the potential power of faith.

Difficult things can happen to us, and it's okay to ask God *why*, but our next words should be, "God help me to see the good that you will do in the midst of this." God is a responsive father, and he wants to be a part of our lives. When we request to see things from his perspective, he is likely to allow us to see outcomes that we will miss if we are not in a faith-filled relationship with him. Frankly, the only way we will know the power and freedom of a life filled with God's presence is when we live life with a faith that is characterized by "positive expectancy." If we want an uncommon joy, peace, and fullness of life, we need to believe God's goodness is going to be revealed in all situations. We need the faith of a child believing that Daddy is working good into all things. When we hold onto this belief, the passing of time will reveal his work, but we blind ourselves to seeing his work when we lack an enduring faith.

Positive Expectancy

A childlike faith at its core is reflected in an attitude of "positive expectancy." This type of faith is remaining expectant of positive outcomes, even if those outcomes are not evident at the moment. Faith says we are so sure about the loving character of God that we only expect good from him. This is what propels us into the type of faith a blessed child of God has, and this is the type of faith that Jesus says we need in order to see the Kingdom of God. As he told his disciples,

> *"I tell you the truth, unless you change and become like little children, you will never enter the kingdom of heaven." Matt. 18:3*

At the very heart of experiencing an active and alive faith has to be the belief that God wants to be in relationship with us. Through a relationship with Jesus by means of the Holy Spirit dwelling within us, God is prepared to bring us into relationship as a son or daughter and walk with us in this life.

> *"Ask and it will be given to you; seek and you will find; knock and the door will be opened to you. For everyone who asks receives; he who seeks finds; and to him who knocks, the door will be opened." Matt. 7:7*

In this verse, Jesus is saying that if we seek God and knock on his door, he will not let us down. This request needs to come from the heart, and fortunately God knows our hearts and will respond to sincere requests for a relationship with him. With a heartfelt request, God opens the door so that we can receive his spiritual input. God is always faithful, and since God is faithful, we can live a life characterized by a childlike, positive expectancy.

Freedom in Faith

Scripture tells us we need faith to please God. Many things can disrupt our faith if we operate our lives with anything less than a wholehearted and far-reaching faith.

> *"And without faith it is impossible to please God. . ." Heb. 11:5*

We can't please God without faith because it is only through faith that we will most clearly experience the life he would like us to have. Around every bend, God wants to show us new aspects to life that we can't see when we have eyes blinded by unbelief and/or a life disconnected from God. When we have eyes that see only what our physical senses allow us to, we miss the bigger narrative of life that God is potentially orchestrating all events in our lives. If he is orchestrating things, then they will turn out as designed.

We should also consider that we live in a broken world with an opposing force of evil, and bad things will happen, but God can use the bad to weave a greater good. Patience is a virtue that allows us to wait and see how events will unfold, knowing we will see God's positive hand of involvement as time moves forward. We need the eyes of a child willing to believe the father is present and active in all things.

> *"Jesus said: 'I tell you the truth, anyone who will not receive the kingdom of God like a little child will never enter it.'" Luke 18:17*

In this verse Jesus is emphasizing that we need the heart of a child to enter the kingdom of God. Have you ever considered that becoming like a spiritual child includes the relinquishment of our deep concerns, cares, and worries? God wants us to experience freedom with the assurance that he is working all things for good. Essentially, we relinquish our cares because when we are in a relationship with God, we believe the Father will take care of us in this life and the life to come. We look for good, release the bad, and positively expect he is walking with us as his children.

Burdens Released

We all seem to be prone to carrying burdens. We do this in part because we do not relinquish our burdens with the level of faith that Jesus and our Father request of us. Too often, we really don't have faith that he will work all things for good. Instead, we carry our burdens, merely hoping things will work out rather than believing things are progressively *being* worked out. Consider that if we really believe he will make all things right, only then are we exercising a childlike faith and doing what Jesus is requesting us to do in the verse below:

"Come to me, all you who are weary and burdened, and I will give you rest. Take my yoke upon you and learn from me, for I am gentle and humble in heart, and you will find rest for your souls. For my yoke is easy and my burden is light." Matt. 11:28

Jesus is requesting that we allow him to carry our burdens because he is certain we will find relief and a newfound freedom when we do. Through faith, we are more likely to see God's hand of involvement in those things we choose to release to him and his purposes.

"Now faith is being sure of what we hope for and certain of what we do not see." Heb. 11:1

"Faith is being sure of what we hope for," because we have faith that our Father is always present and orchestrating things for good. This knowledge gives us perpetual hope and continual assurances. Furthermore, we are "certain of what we do not see" because we have faith that we will eventually see good in final outcomes because the Father is at work.

Joy Through Relationship

Just what is God's will for us in our childlike, positively expectant faith relationship with him?

"Be joyful always; pray continually; give thanks in all circumstances, for this is God's will for you in Christ Jesus." 1 Thess. 5:16–18

In evaluating this verse, "pray continually" means to be in communication with God at all times. This is only possible through the indwelling of the Holy Spirit. The Holy Spirit is the third, equal person of the Trinity. When the Spirit enters us, we are then specially wired to be in communication with the Father and the Son, through the Holy Spirit. When the Holy Spirit enters us, this union with the Trinity gives us a chance at an indwelling peace, which as the verse above says, allows us to "be joyful always."

Through God's presence in us, we are intended to experience the joy of a child knowing that Daddy is listening and making all things good. Through this childlike faith, we can "give thanks in all circumstances." Finally, it says that all of this is ours because this is "God's will for you." It is God's will for us to know Jesus, be filled with the Spirit, and to live within a reality not governed by sight but by faith. We gain eyes for the Kingdom's work if we see all things with faith, knowing that the Father will bring good, even in the challenges of life. There is pain in our fallen world, but faith allows us to rise above the pain because of our confidence in an indwelling, all-knowing, and all-powerful God who says he wants to be our Abba (Daddy).

Life Story

After reading this chapter, you are aware that Jesus said it takes a childlike faith to experience the kingdom of God. I have to say I was fortunate that my first real introduction to the faith was as a child, with a childlike openness. I was 13 years old when my parents took me to an event at our local event center in the city of Midland, Michigan. The person speaking was Harold Hill, and he had written a book called *How to Live Like a King's Kid*. Mr. Hill talked about his faith in Jesus and the miraculous events in his life that he attributed to a living relationship with Jesus. I bought his book and read it. I was young enough to believe that I also could be one of the "Kids of the King."

A few months later I was pushed into trusting God, and He responded in very personal and dramatically specific ways. One afternoon while at home, I had a sudden onset of excessive internal bleeding that was showing up when I went to the toilet, so I was taken to the hospital. The cause of the bleeding event had the doctors stumped. They lined up multiple medical tests to try to examine my inner workings and discover the source of it. Some of the tests were very painful. Today, sedation would be used for a couple of these tests, but apparently in that era no sedation was used because it wasn't provided for me at that time. The bleeding was what sent me to the hospital for all these tests, but the bleeding had stopped within hours of being admitted.

The second day of being in the hospital, I was in my hospital bed by myself—my parents had taken a break from being confined to the hospital with me. During this time, a member of the hospital staff came into the room and said they were to prepare me for surgery. They could tell from my shock that this was news to me, and the nurse left the room to verify their orders. They came back shortly and said they had made a mistake. I might have been a kid but that was not a minor mistake and it put some fear into me. Not long after this a doctor came in and announced they had another test planned for the afternoon.

I felt alone and scared of the new tortures they had planned. Out of fear and self-defense, I started to pray. I prayed for no more tests today, and within minutes of the prayer a nurse came back in the room and said the doctors changed their minds and were not going to do any more tests today, but they would likely have a couple more tests tomorrow. Seeing that the first prayer worked, I quickly prayed that they would not do any tests tomorrow either. Just a short time later the nurse came and said they were dropping the tests planned for tomorrow, but they wanted to keep me there for observation to make sure the problem did not recur. Again, the previous two prayers seemed to work, so immediately I decided to pray that I could go home. Not long after this prayer they came in and announced they had decided I could go home as soon as my parents returned to sign me out.

The doctors made it clear that whatever caused the bleeding could happen again, at any point in time. Feeling rather confident that God was listening and answering my prayers, I prayed out of fear and desperation that this would never happen to me again. Five decades later this bleeding has never recurred. Honestly, I wonder if the entire event was allowed to happen to me so that I could learn to rely on God and begin walking on the path of childlike belief with a positive expectancy that God can work all things for good.

I prayed and He answered when I was only thirteen years old, and I still believe He is attentive to my thoughts and prayers to this day. The series of three answered prayers in the hospital as a child seemed to set a precedent for further communication with God in my life. Decades have passed, but he still often verifies his presence in my life by using signs in a series of three. As my time and relationship with God have grown, I also believe I have grown more sensitive to the inward voice of the Holy Spirit. Currently in my walk with God, signs in the form of triplicates are not as necessary to understand God's presence in a situation, but answers in the form of three are still less likely to escape my attention. When God does reveal his presence to me in triplicates I just kind of laugh and let him know I am grateful for the obvious communication.

It may not be in the form of threes, but God speaks to each of us personally in different ways. Like a good parent, God knows his children and how to speak to them effectively. Are you aware of how God communicates with you as a "Kid of the King"? Even more importantly, have you accepted Christ into your life so you have been adopted into this relationship?

Questions for Reflection

Was there a concept or statement in this chapter that struck you the most? What was it? Explain why.

What is the first thing that comes to your mind when you consider what might prevent you from feeling "childlike" in your faith?

Do you think this barrier is self-constructed? If so, why and how?

What persistent worries do you have? Do you think worry and faith are compatible in any way?

As God's child, do you believe you can live with a continual "positive expectancy" in God? If so, what do you envision this looking like?

CHAPTER 2

Relational Gratitude

Interwoven Faith and Gratitude

IN THE PREVIOUS CHAPTER we reflected on the topic of faith and examined some different Scriptures related to it. With all of the topics we discuss within this book, it is important we realize that we more than likely set boundaries on our beliefs that fall short of God's Truth. If we are seeking the truth about any element of our lives, we have to learn how God views it. If we hold any view that is outside of God's view of reality, then we hold onto some degree of falsehood. For instance, if we believe in murdering innocent people, we hold a view that is in direct opposition to our God of love. How about the question, "Does God care about all of our prayers?" The answer to this is not as clear, but the truth is if we reach any belief that is not in alignment with God's view of reality, then we are operating out of false beliefs. The topic of faith in the previous chapter was partly intended to bring to the surface the possibility that our level of faith operates outside of the truth God wants us to live within. Ponder for a moment that gratitude is interwoven with and inseparable from faith. If you truly have faith, then you will be truly grateful. Therefore, understanding gratitude is paramount in evaluating our level of faith.

To do a brief recap of a couple of thoughts from the last chapter, we used the analogy of a child on the edge of the swimming pool who was afraid to jump into the deep water. Yet this fear was overcome by the child's faith in her father's waiting arms. To be like the child we need to believe our heavenly Father is fully trustworthy for our leap of faith to be secure. We have to ask ourselves: do we believe he is fully engaged in all aspects of our lives, part of it, or none of it? If we lack faith we need to determine who we have made our God out to be, and if we have falsely created him in our own image rather than seeing him for who he truly is. Perhaps we need to also consider if the level of God's engagement in our lives is reflective of our effort to engage with him. Consider the verse below in regard to this reciprocal relationship:

> *Jesus said, "Come near to God and he will come near to you." Luke 4:8*

As part of this evaluation of faith we looked at Jesus' words about yielding ourselves like a child:

> *"I tell you the truth, anyone who will not receive the kingdom of God like a little child will never enter it." Luke 18:17*

We also see in Hebrews that we can't please our father without faith:

> *"And without faith it is impossible to please God." Heb. 11:5*

To see God for who he is and to understand the truth about him, we also need to have faith that once we give our lives to him, he can orchestrate all this life's events, and he *is* potentially actively at work in all things:

> *"And we know that in all things God works for the good of those who love him, who have been called according to his purpose." Rom. 8:28*

Understand that the apostle Paul was imprisoned in Rome as he penned the words, "that in all things God works for the good of those who love him." Those are bold words of faith for a man in prison because of his faith in Jesus. Like Paul, if we are living out our faith with the assuredness of a child, with full confidence in our Father, we should display and reflect it through expressions of faith and gratitude.

Boxes of Faith

Because faith and gratitude are woven together, we need to look more carefully at the concept of gratitude. Gratitude is an outward expression of an inward state of being. If we have drawn boundary lines on God's character and limit our faith because of our imaginary boundaries, then our expression of gratitude will also be dictated by the size of our self-determined "boxes of faith." Frankly, we become restrained by our own errors of beliefs. Certainly, each of our minds have created some limitations on our scope of faith, and this simultaneously affects our experience and expression of gratitude. It is important to keep in mind just what God's perspective of reality is because anything outside of this is simply our perspective, and our perspectives will vary in degrees of truth depending on how far off we are from God's view of reality.

The Power of Gratitude

To gain more of God's perspective on the importance of faith and gratitude, let's look at aspects of the life of King David. The biblical character David was the youngest of many brothers, and he was merely a shepherd boy when he entered a battle with Goliath. He defeated the giant because of his faith. David believed God was great, and present, and would use him to defeat this great enemy. God did just that! We learn from Scripture that God gave David high praise for his faith in action:

> *"After removing Saul, he made David their king. He testified concerning him: 'I have found David son of Jesse **a man after my own heart**; he will do everything I want him to do.'" Acts 13:22*

If we consider the statement that David was a "man after God's own heart," then we should look at what makes God feel this way about David. If we are supposed to be men and women after God's own heart, then what does this look like for us?

We already saw that David had courage in the face of a life-and-death situation with Goliath. This courage was only possible because of David's sold-out faith. Just as Jesus suggested we need a childlike faith to see and experience the kingdom of God, this childlike faith allowed David to see and believe the kingdom of God was at work all around him. In his heart, David trusted God was alive and active and at work in all things, even fighting a giant with a sling and a stone. As you study the life of David, all the things he did within his relationship with God turned out well but all the things he did outside of this relationship had dire consequences. David made huge mistakes. At the top of the list was the intentional murder of a friend, after David had impregnated the friend's wife while his friend was away fighting a battle for David. In order for David to hold the prestigious award of being a man after God's own heart, there had to be something very significant that outweighed all his other faults.

I submit that this "something else" David had was an overwhelming faith in God along with a repentant heart. Consider that if you cannot be pleasing to God without faith, then it would seem logical that David would have to have demonstrated an unparalleled faith to earn the title of a man after God's own heart. So, what can we learn from his character that would help make us men and women after God's own heart? First, faith is overwhelmingly evident in David's writings, and this faith is often expressed in gratitude. When considering David's words that express gratitude, several pop out: *thanksgiving, praise,* and *rejoice.* If the Bible is a book divinely orchestrated as a manual to be used in guiding our lives toward God's Truth, then let's take seriously the fact that the word *praise* is used 420 times in the NIV edition of the Bible; the word *rejoice* is used 191 times; and the words *thanks* and *thanksgiving* appear 133 times. Without a doubt, a large concentration of these words were written by David as a reflection of his faith and love in a God who became very personal to him. Because thanksgiving, praise, and rejoicing all are an outpouring of the faith contained within our hearts, we also need to be aware that

discontentment, worry, and grumbling are potentially as disheart-
ening to God as a childlike faith is beautiful to him.

The following verses from David's pen gives us a glimpse of
His faith and gratitude:

> *I will exalt you, my God the King; I will praise your name*
> *for ever and ever. Psalms 145:1*

> *The LORD is my strength and my shield; my heart trusts*
> *in him, and I am helped. My heart leaps for joy and I will*
> *give thanks to him in song. Psalms 28:7*

> *Praise the LORD. Give thanks to the LORD, for he is good;*
> *his love endures forever. Psalms 106:1*

> *I will give thanks to the LORD because of his righteousness*
> *and will sing praise to the name of the LORD Most High.*
> *Psalms 7:17*

> *Praise be to God, who has not rejected my prayer or with-*
> *held his love from me! Psalms 66:20*

Faith in Action

For a Christian who unconditionally believes the following verse,
it stands to reason that potentially every aspect of every day is part
of God's work in our lives:

> *"And we know that in all things God works for the good of*
> *those who love him, who have been called according to his*
> *purpose." Romans 8:28*

If we have faith that God sincerely wants good for us in all
circumstances, then it only makes sense that we should have our
eyes wide open, looking for outcomes to be grateful for. This way
of thinking goes against most of our natures, so it may be difficult
to step out of our normal way of viewing things to see God's work
in our lives and the world around us. Gratitude is a choice, so the
more we choose to look at life through a lens of gratitude, the more
natural it will become for us. Consider that the opposite to expressions of gratitude is grumbling. It is also true that grumbling and

ungratefulness not only have spiritual implications but physical and emotional consequences as well. Grumbling and ungratefulness trap us into an existence that is manifested by poor health, empty hearts, and no hope.

No doubt, life will dish out challenging times. Having a gratitude-oriented faith does not mean we have to like the difficult things in life, but it does mean we believe God can and *will* make good come from them. Often the good that comes from difficulties is God's cultivation of a more mature and useful child, so that we in turn can help other children grow in their walk of faith. Just as our earthly parents knew that sometimes the best lessons for growth come through difficulties, our heavenly Father certainly knows this as well. Walking with the Father is not living life in a fully protective bubble from any and all of life's hardships, but there is an assuredness that trials will often produce tangible benefits because we have faith the Father is present and orchestrating outcomes. The point is, do we believe God is active in difficulties, even in seemingly tragic events of life? Hopeful children would say "Yes" because they fully trust their Father. A hopeful child will also see positive outcomes the grumbler will never see because the ungrateful mind and eyes have been closed to this perspective, God's perspective.

How is Your Gratitude

When we look at gratitude as a reflection of faith, we really need to start with an evaluation of the thoughts that cross our minds and the words that come out of our mouths. If we are characterized by doubt, worry, and grumbling, I submit that we are living in a reality outside of where God would like us to be. If we are born-again children of God with the Holy Spirit indwelling us, then there is a very different reality available for us to experience if we have the bold faith of a child. Sadly, those who set their own boundaries and limits on faith shut down the capacity to see beyond their own self-determined walls. Unquestionably, Jesus turned the belief systems of mankind upside down in many ways. This is as true today as it was then, and it may be hard to grasp God's/Jesus' view of reality because it is frequently contrary to our preconceived notions.

The Way

Jesus Christ came to earth, was crucified, and was raised from the dead for the forgiveness of our sins. Through him we can be granted the gift of spending eternity within God's heavenly kingdom. Jesus said the entrance into heaven is dependent on a relationship with him and only after we have invited him into our lives. Through this relationship God opens the door for the Holy Spirit to live within us. Perhaps you haven't heard this before, but Jesus did not actually come to start a new religion. Jesus came to start a relationship with anyone who is drawn by the Holy Spirit to him and who has the faith to believe Jesus is the way, the truth, and the light.

> *Jesus said, "I am the way and the truth and the life. No one comes to the Father except through me." John 14:6*

Perhaps we are missing out on more abundant, joyful, and hopeful lives because our "box of faith" is too small to allow us to experience more fullness in our relationship to God. Perhaps King David experienced more gratitude because he had more faith—a faith that expected good to come from any circumstance because God was involved. Too often we are not grateful because we somehow fall out of the belief that God can, and is, orchestrating things. Have you asked God to orchestrate your days? If so, do you truly believe he is doing so? Full submission through faith and expressions of gratitude opens our eyes to the possibility that every event has the potential for God's involvement.

Hopefully, we have all experienced God's orchestration of some really inspiring situations and events in our lives. But are we really seeing the majority of his activity in our daily lives? Are we expectant of his continual presence? Grumbling says God is not right and God is not in control. Gratitude, on the other hand, leaves our hearts and minds open to God's hand in everything, even in the unpleasant or difficult times. God's beauty and workmanship are unsurpassed, and continual gratitude helps us see the activity of God because we are always anticipating good, even if we can't see it in the moment. Could it be that ongoing, unconditional gratitude allows us to experience more of God because it opens our mind's eye to seeing beyond the barriers of doubt?

> *"Give thanks in all circumstances, for this is God's will for*
> *you in Christ Jesus." 1 Thess. 5:18*

We are to "give thanks in all circumstance" because if you have invited Jesus into all aspects of your life then expect that he is at work.

Freedom for the Heart

Not long ago I walked by a daycare center where kids were outside running, playing, and laughing in the sunshine. They had a mental and emotional freedom that most of us lose as adults. Yes, I observed childish/immature behavior, but more so there was an observable, childlike faith shining through them that says, "All is good in life!" Through faith we have the potential, at any age, to experience more of the heartfelt freedom of a child. This is not childish in the immature sense; rather, it is what God would like for his children to experience. I believe Scripture supports this view of reality, but we will never experience it as our personal reality unless we jump into it, just as a child jumps with faith into their father's arms.

> *"Let us hold unswervingly to the hope we profess, for he*
> *who promised is faithful." Heb. 10:23*

The challenge here is not to say, "Okay God, if you show me all the good you will do, then I will have faith." No. God simply wants us to step forward with faith, believing that he *will* show us his presence and his power as we believe in him. No doubt another thing God loved about David was the way he stepped into and embraced God's plans, believing that God would make it ultimately turn out for good. God does not promise an easy ride, but he does promise a fulfilling one. So, friends, be grateful and have faith.

Life Story

The following life story is here because, while we can be grateful for many things in this life, without question the thing that should be number one on our gratitude list is God's attempts to draw us near to him and provide an eternal destiny in His Kingdom. The phrase, "attitude of gratitude" is very simple, but I believe within it are the keys to living and seeing our world with a Kingdom perspective—a perspective that is very different from the world's.

An experience in my early twenties cemented my belief in God's continual presence. It was one of the most profoundly miraculous moments of my life, yet it happened when I felt all alone and in a spiritually dark setting. It all began after returning from several days of being immersed in the presence of the Holy Spirit at a Christian men's retreat where I believe I was "officially" born-again. I say officially because I believe God had been walking with me and drawing me near to him since my youth as illustrated by the story in the previous chapter. Yet it was at this retreat that I fully invited God into my life through a relationship with Jesus Christ, and I was baptized as a sign of this new relationship.

When I returned from the retreat on a Saturday night, I was alone in my apartment in Ann Arbor, Michigan (while attending the University of Michigan). The weekend had been filled with other like-minded men and the presence of the Holy Spirit. Now that I was back at my apartment, I felt alone in an environment that seemed spiritually empty. In this moment, I made a late-night request to Jesus and his Father, asking that I would have someone to be with that night so that I would not feel so isolated. Within a minute of this prayer, the phone rang and a professing atheist friend of mine asked me to walk a few blocks to his home and play a game of Backgammon. I said yes because the timing of this call could not have been anything other than a rather odd answer to my prayer to have someone to be with. This call was the beginning of a night filled with miraculous events that still remain vivid in my mind's eye today.

If you are unfamiliar with the game of Backgammon, essentially it is a game that involves a little bit of strategy, but mostly luck—you simply roll dice to move your pieces around the board in order to win. I don't ever remember beating this friend in Backgammon before, and I was losing miserably when I told God in that moment that it was odd He had this particular friend call. Due to his atheistic worldview, this friend would never understand the spiritual high I had experienced over the weekend, and thus I could not share my experience with him. Because of this, I felt spiritually alone even while in his company. Plus, I was losing the game!

Then I asked God to let me know he was there, to give me a sign of his presence. From that request on, except for one, every roll of the dice I made resulted in doubles. If you roll a double in Backgammon, you get to roll again. My friend could not believe what he was seeing, and he was getting a little upset that he was going to lose to someone with unusually annoying luck. Eventually it came to my final roll of the dice in which I would win the game. But something unexpected and unexplainable happened. During this final roll, one of the dice spun on its end for approximately ten seconds, but when it finally stopped spinning, it did not fall over like dice always do. Rather, it was standing on its rounded end and did not fall over at all!

My friend went crazy seeing this dice standing on end, so he got up from the table to get his camera in order to capture this highly unusual event. To his dismay, he had no film in the camera. For any younger readers, this was a time before digital cameras and you had to have film to capture a picture. If you were out of film, you were out of options for a picture. My mind immediately felt he had no film in his camera because this event was for me alone to remember, and it was not intended to be captured on film. He then picked up the dice that was still standing and inspected the corner it was standing on. He exclaimed, "It's round!" which would make the dice standing on its end a virtual impossibility. After several attempts of trying to get it to stand on end again, he gave up.

Now that the game was over I was ready to leave as it was past midnight and my body and soul were now ready for a peaceful night's sleep. But aside from rolling doubles one after another and then having the dice stand on its end on my final roll, God had one more sign to confirm his presence. As a final confirmation, my friend pointed to a colorfully wrapped present on his dresser and mockingly said, "Get a load of this! I am supposed to deliver it to someone for their wedding gift." It was the wrapping paper he was mocking, and the paper had images of open Holy Bibles all over it. All I could do is smile and walk home knowing God was right there with me.

My request for companionship that night was not fulfilled by my friend, but by the presence of the Lord. As far as the dice standing on end, perhaps it was an angel that held its finger on the dice to keep it from falling? The fact that my friend could get up from the table and walk across an old wood floor to get his camera without causing the dice to fall is simply not explainable in a natural physical reality. Perhaps in heaven I will learn more of what was going on in that room. To be sure, God's three distinct answers to my request to let me know he was present were a wonderful gift that I am forever grateful for. My life has been filled with enough direct communication and answers to prayer that I simply could never deny him.

How often do we ask God to be a part of our lives, yet we miss his answers because we don't really believe that he is going to respond? Or how often do we miss seeing God at work because his answers are not what we wanted or expected? This event left me extremely grateful for a God who can show us visual signs when we yearn for the confirmation of his presence. I would have to have been dumb as a brick to miss seeing his presence in this situation, but we do need spiritual eyes to see and spiritual ears to hear if we are to walk in a living and vital relationship with the Trinity.

Questions on Gratitude

Was there a concept or statement in this chapter that struck you most? Explain why.

Is your life characterized by gratitude towards God? Why or why not?

Would you agree that faith and gratitude are interwoven? If so, how?

What are barriers that keep you from living a life of faith and gratitude?

In your life, which areas of your beliefs/values do you feel match God's perspective of reality?

Are there areas in your life that could use more of God's perspective? Explain.

CHAPTER 3

Walls and the Will

T HIS CHAPTER'S TOPIC FOLLOWS the previous studies on Faith
and Gratitude because our faith and hence our level of gratitude toward God are likely to be limited by boundaries or walls
that we have set in place regarding our understanding of who, and
what, God is. At best, we understand God in simple ways, yet we
define much of our existence based on a level of ignorance of who
God is, and thus we limit who he can be in our daily lives.

Forming Our God

Unfortunately, no matter how educated we are regarding Scripture, we still falsely place boundaries on God. We do this for an
endless array of reasons, and each of our reasons may be somewhat unique. For instance, our upbringing and our experience
with our own human parental figures often start to form some
of the walls and limitations we put on God. Pastors I know who
work directly with youth who have experienced abusive fathers
often purposely leave God, "The Father," out of their terminology
and instead introduce Jesus as "The Brother" as a starting point
of introducing them to the Bible. They do this to provide a sense
of emotional safety by not evoking negative images associated
with the word father. The tendency to associate God with human
figures of authority can begin the wall-building process. Other
foundational pieces to our walls may be bad personal experiences
where we believe God failed us. The walls and boundaries we

place on God are very likely falsehoods we have come to believe, and our faith is crippled because of them.

Wall Building

Many of our barriers to knowing God may be self-determined, but we also are engaged in spiritual battles. To be sure, Satan will use whatever tricks he can to build walls to keep us from experiencing a trusting, faith-filled relationship with Jesus and his Father. Many people, whether they want to acknowledge it or not, are reluctant to enter into a fully intimate relationship with God. This reluctance of forming a relationship with God can stem from a concern about being accountable, which would likely require shifts in lifestyles and behaviors that a person is unwilling to give up. Certainly, if power figures in our lives have been unsafe, this fear can be transferred to the ultimate power figure as well. Out of all our walls, pride is most likely the hardest wall to tear down because our pride can mentally shut out God with little or no room for new information. As the Psalmist wrote:

> *"In his pride the wicked does not seek him; in all his thoughts there is no room for God." Ps. 10:4*

Our Restrictive Boxes of Faith

We start life with a sin nature, but relatively free of many of the walls and barriers to faith that will come from many sources as we grow older. We do have the potential to grow in a childlike faith with fewer and less rigid walls—but all walls keep us from a flourishing relationship with our Creator. Unfortunately, most of us grow up in environments that create barriers to living in the childlike freedom that God intended for his creation. Too often, as the years pass, the openness to life we experienced as a child gets replaced by walls, barriers, and falsely contrived restrictions toward God. The bottom line is that we all create walls around our belief systems, and this is especially true when it comes to who God is. We make God into our image, and we lose the childlike faith it takes to see and experience God for who he truly is.

Building a Box

In my early 20's I worked on a custom home building crew. As part of the building sequence we were able to start framing for the walls once the foundation was completed and the plywood floor was in place. The walls were framed one-by-one while lying on the wood floor. Once the framed wall was complete, we would stand it up and fasten it to the floor, and then adjacent walls were framed, stood up, and fastened together. Eventually all the walls were up and fastened in place so the roof could then be constructed. With this visual in mind, consider for a moment how we all tend to build walls of belief and disbelief about God so that we feel safe in our own box of beliefs. Everyone's walls may be different, but we all build them to one degree or another.

Let's look at some common walls we may create that trap us into boxes of unbelief. The "God Isn't" wall is a common wall of disbelief, and it puts false parameters on God by restricting God to limitations that really don't exist for him. The idea that God isn't all powerful or all-knowing are common walls for many. Another wall that makes up some of our boxes is the "God Doesn't" wall. "God doesn't love me and watch over me" is another common theme in many lives. This wall of doubt is self-contrived and is not based on God's view of reality. A third wall can be a "God Won't" wall. "God won't do this or do that in my life" combined with the previous walls of God Doesn't and God Isn't are creating barriers that become difficult if not impossible to break down. Again, Jesus warns us all that unless we can become as children and drop our self-imposed walls, we will not be able to see him and his Father through the barriers we have formed. Another potential wall is the "God Can't" wall. This wall directly opposes a life of faith and shuts down the power associated with believing.

If you are following my progression of thought, four walls have now been erected. God Isn't, God Doesn't, God Won't, and

God Can't walls create barriers to seeing the truth of who God is, and they interfere with our ability to have a living and vital relationship with him. But the good news is, even with these four walls, the top of the box is still open. Although the walls create barriers to seeing outside of our self-constructed boxes, there is still hope that God the Father, Jesus, and the Spirit can gain access to our hearts and minds from above.

However, the last part of building a fully enclosed box is the roof. If we put a roof on this metaphorically open box, we ultimately say, "God Does Not Exist." This is particularly sad since it completely closes the box off to God. No access point to God means no room for a relationship with the infinite mind of our Creator. It is very ironic that many atheists who try to seal themselves off from God feel they are openminded and enlightened people, when in actuality they have closed themselves off from the mind of the infinite. They exist merely within their own minds, which is a very small box of existence indeed.

We all erect various walls of limitations on God, and this restricts life to a narrower reality than what God created and intended. God is infinite, yet we limit him out of disbelief, fear, pride, and a host of other reasons. We do not live in the fullest form of reality without God; we live in a distorted reality when we limit this divine relationship. If you choose to withhold belief that God wants to be in relationship with you, or that he is not all knowing and all powerful as Scripture promises, then you currently have walls that hinder knowing him. What wall have you put up that limits God's working in your life? Where in your life are you relying on your own beliefs rather than experiencing God's view of reality?

Who is God?

The things that create walls between us and God are nearly endless. It is my hope that as we proceed we at least get a glimpse of walls we have constructed from our finite understanding of God and how these might limit God and thus limit our experience of his fullness. The truth is, we self-create many of our falsehoods and inherit some from other sources.

> *Jesus said to his disciples: "Do you still not see or under-stand? Are your hearts hardened? Do you have eyes but fail to see, and ears but fail to hear?" Mark 8: 17–18*

Undoubtedly, our concepts of God will fall dramatically short of who he actually is. The truth be told, our human minds can't fathom him no matter what. This is, in part, because we have no similar reference point to compare God to. For instance, we live in a world based on matter (physical things), and all things in our world undergo decay (they break down and go away). God is outside of all of this, so our finite existence provides few valid points of reference for understanding the eternal nature of God. In addition, God is a spiritual being, likely without shape as we know it. The fact that God is not physical by nature creates a bar-rier of understanding because we are surrounded by a world of sight, sounds, taste, and touch.

Amazingly, God is a person and spiritual being who is ca-pable of creating matter (physical things), yet he is not restricted to physical form himself and is capable of being in all places at the same time. His omnipresence would not be possible if he was in any type of permanent physical state. We know by definition that God is spirit, but he is a spirit that is capable of creating physical things, and he is the creative force behind all that we see and touch. We can review, speculate, and hypothesize some of these attributes of God, but fully understanding them is not possible from our lim-ited state of being. The extent of God is not knowable and hence any boundaries we set on him are likely to be distorted or outright false. The following scriptures testify to this:

> *"The God who made the world and everything in it is the Lord of heaven and earth and does not live in temples built by hands." Acts 17:24*

> *"For by him all things were created: things in heaven and on earth, visible and invisible, whether thrones or powers*

or rulers or authorities; all things were created by him and for him." Col. 1:16

"To whom, then, will you compare God? What image will you compare him to?" Is. 40:18

Limiting God

If you are intrigued by the wild concepts of things portrayed in fiction such as Star Trek, Star Wars, Lord of the Rings, and the array of immortal Marvel movie characters, then you could be a step closer to considering God. Only our wildest imaginations might begin to grasp what and who he is. Whether expressed as the gods of Greek mythology or our modern-day super-hero movies, humans sense the presence of the spirit world that surrounds us. We conjure up supernatural thoughts, not because spiritual beings don't exist, but because they do exist. We are spiritual beings, housed in limited physical bodies for a time. Built within us is a knowledge that there is something more, something eternal, something outside of ourselves. We have an indwelling sense within us that says there is more beyond what our eyes can see.

It is my hope that we all stay open to what this something more may be and that we tear down some of the walls that minimize our existence and interfere with our faith. It also is extremely important to keep in mind that truth is only truth if it is in alignment with God's perspective of reality. As we explore our walls, we need to continually ask ourselves if the walls we have made restrict the size of our God and define a limited level of faith. An appropriate question for each of us is this: are our self-determined walls in alignment with God's perspective of reality? In other words, would God agree with who you have made him out to be?

There are things we know about God, but there are far more aspects of him that we don't know. God has given us enough information about himself through Scripture to know that he desires a relationship with us. He provided a path to eternity through his son Jesus, and it is through a relationship with his son we receive his Spirit and gain entrance to eternity with God. God knows we can't handle all that he is because he is beyond our comprehension. Through Jesus, God made himself man so we can identify with something tangible, human, physical, and in one sense finite.

We all resort to creating a God in the best image we can conjure up, but it will never fully represent him. Often, the walls we place on God are there to create some form of comfort for ourselves, but if we truly had the faith of a child perhaps we would find out that our walls blind us from what is beyond them: something glorious.

> *"How great is God—beyond our understanding! The number of his years is past finding out." Job 36:26*

Walls of Religion and Tradition

The Pharisees were the dominant religious leaders of Jesus' day, and they had constructed such rigid boxes of belief that they became hard-hearted and spiritually blind. To the Pharisees Jesus said:

> *"You hypocrites! Isaiah was right when he prophesied about you: 'These people honor me with their lips, but their hearts are far from me. They worship me in vain; their teachings are but rules taught by men.'" Matt 15:7–9*

Without a doubt, we have a great example of wall-building in the religious leaders of Jesus' day. The Pharisees were the most knowledgeable of their Holy Scriptures which foretold the coming of the Christ (Messiah). Like most of us, they created boundaries around what the Christ (God) would behave like when he came. When Christ did come, they did not accept him because he was outside of the lines they had drawn in their own minds and traditions. The very people anxious for Christ's appearing could not see him because of their preconceived boundaries. If Christ came back today, would we accept him? Would we recognize him through our own walls? Most certainly he would not come as a Republican or Democrat.

Jesus consistently came against people and religious traditions that distorted, or led people astray from knowing, the true nature of his Father. From what is written in Scripture, Jesus appears to largely stay out of cultural and political matters of his day that were not directly associated with spiritual issues of faith. No doubt, the oppression of the Roman government, pagan worship, rampant prostitution, and the Roman male elites use of young boys for sexual purposes had to be disturbing to Jesus. Despite these things, Jesus' focus was on those who searched in their hearts for the one true God. Anyone, or anything, that diverted people from properly understanding the Father evoked Jesus's rebukes.

Undoubtedly, today there are different religious traditions and beliefs within the denominations of Christianity that would also irritate Jesus. If Jesus rebuked religious leaders of his day for placing powers in the hands of men rather than God, then he would certainly rebuke many of the priests, pastors, and various religious leaders of our day as well. The question is, would we recognize and acknowledge Christ if he did not appear in the image we have created for him?

Boundaries and the Will

Another important thought in all of this is how our will is tied into our self-constructed boundaries. Our will, which allows us to choose a relationship with God, is also what defines some of the boundaries we place on our understanding of God. Remember, if truth is God's perspective of reality, then knowing God's will is part of knowing his truth. Once we are in relationship with God through Jesus, the Holy Spirit desires us to direct our will more and more into alignment with God's will.

Transforming our wills generally happens through life lessons and experiences that God uses to shape us. Our will either opens up to God and is allowed to be transformed, or it shuts down and limits God. We cannot harden our hearts and defy God without expecting consequences:

"They are darkened in their understanding and separated from the life of God because of the ignorance that is in them due to the hardening of their hearts." Eph. 4:18

The Apostle Paul

Our self-determined wills certainly govern many of our paths in this life, including the level of relationship we have with God. Fortunately, our wills don't always get the final say in our lives, and God puts us in situations designed to bend our wills to conform to realities that we would never experience without his hand of involvement. The Apostle Paul is a good example of God bending a will into conformity"

"Paul, an apostle of Christ Jesus by the will of God." Eph. 1:1

"An apostle of Christ Jesus *by the will of God*" is certainly an accurate statement regarding Paul. Paul had a very strong will to do what was right in God's eyes, but before he met Christ he was blinded by false beliefs which put God in a box that was completely out of phase with God's will. Paul experienced an undeniable experience on the road to the city of Damascus. He saw a great light, heard from Christ directly, was blinded, and had to be led by others to Damascus. Through this experience, Paul's will was brought into submission to God's view of reality. Prior to God's intervention, Paul was seeking out, imprisoning, and killing Christians. In no uncertain terms, Paul was what we would consider a religious terrorist. Once the Holy Spirit entered Paul, his will was transformed, and rather than killing the followers of Jesus, he became Christ's greatest witness. Paul points out that it was by God's will that he became an apostle of Christ. However, even with this radical experience Paul still had a choice to follow Jesus or not. This was said to Paul when he was healed from his blindness:

*"The God of our fathers has chosen you to know his will and to see the Righteous One and to hear words from his mouth. You will be his witness to all men of what you have seen and heard. **And now what are you waiting for?** Get*

up, be baptized and wash your sins away, calling on his name." Acts 22: 14–16

The statement "And now what are you waiting for?" indicates Paul still had a decision to make: to follow God's will or his own. Although Paul's experience was dramatic, I bet most of us have had direct experiences with God's hand of provision in our lives. Yet by our own doubts and disbeliefs we have pushed those events aside, and we persist in creating boundaries that don't include the expectation of God's regular activity in our lives. It would be my guess that we see only a fraction of God's participation in our lives because of our lack of faith. We don't live with the positive expectancy of a child, so, just as Christ suggested, we don't see the kingdom of God at work. Our self-constructed walls too often block our view of God's presence.

Life Story

An unfortunate part of our walls and barriers is how they can restrict our minds and spirits from seeing God's activity. As I write this, in the last twelve hours I have been reminded that he can speak to us in many ways, including dreams, but we must have our walls down to believe he can and possibly will do this in our lives. Personally, I dream every night, but most of my dreams are forgotten as soon as they end or as soon as I wake up. On occasion, I will have a dream vivid enough that it imprints itself on my heart. After such a dream, my mind/spirit replays the content of the dream repeatedly. I have learned that these types of dreams need further consideration as to the source and the reason for the dream.

Interestingly, many people believe their dreams may be telling them something, but they don't attribute the source of the dream to the spirit realm. It's not unusual for someone who claims to have no spiritual beliefs to ask a friend whether his or her dream might have an underlying meaning. Honestly, we can't put credence in our dreams if they simply come from the workings of our own minds, but they can mean something much more significant if they come from a spiritual source outside of ourselves.

From personal experience, these more vivid dreams are impactful enough to my spirit that I hold on to the possibility that something more is going on and my dream may be revealing or forecasting something. I've seen from past experiences that some of my more vivid dreams come as warnings of events that are currently taking place in life around me. These dreams are usually put together in odd ways, as most dreams are, so interpreting them can be a bit puzzling. Yet as the truth of the dream unfolds in real life, so does the meaning of the dream.

For example, last night I had a dream that involved a group of Christian brothers whom I have met with at least monthly for the past 20 years. The dream involved marital unfaithfulness, but I was unable to discern specifics from the dream. The only sense I had from this dream was that within this group something was not right in regard to marital faithfulness. As I went to work that morning, the dream kept coming to my mind. I felt repeatedly prompted to send an email to the group regarding the dream. Out of respect for privacy in this matter, I wrote the note in a way to leave an open door for conversation, without disclosing the subject matter of the dream. This was my note:

> Hello Men,
>
> This email may be completely irrelevant, and it may seem a little odd, but occasionally I get dreams that are more detailed, and aspects of them I can't immediately get out of my mind. In the past many of these dreams have been part of things unseen to me at the moment. Well, I had a dream last night about our NEBS group and I won't explain it, but if any of you have something in life you want a private ear to talk about, I am available if you need or want it.
>
> Peace,
> B

Within thirty minutes of the email going out, I got an email back from a brother in the group asking me to call him. We arranged to talk after my workday was complete. He told me that last night he had been praying to God for someone with whom to share his life situation. He proceeded to tell me that his wife had asked for a separation, and that he was concerned about her being unfaithful.

My dream was simply a notification that something was going on, but I had to take the time to believe it might have been the Spirit's prompting. I stuck my neck out a bit knowing that some in the group might think I had gone a little bonkers by believing my dream was really about someone in the group. I also knew that I was potentially making more out of the dream than reality called for. Yet I believe the Holy Spirit kept bringing the dream to my mind so not only would I not ignore its content, but that I would also take some form of action regarding it. My brother needed a listening ear in a trying time, and the Spirit prompted my participation through a vivid dream.

You might think this is an odd subject in a chapter about walls, but perhaps we miss God's communication because we put up walls that simply say, "God can't . . . God won't . . . God isn't . . . " For instance, do you personally rule out communication from God through a dream of your own? Walls are often made to defend our limited view of reality, and in the process they can also create blindness to a spiritual existence beyond our walls. No doubt, most of the communication from the Trinity will come from reading Scripture and through the words of people around us, but dreams can also be part of God's way of speaking to us. If our minds will not release a thought or the contents of an impactful dream, perhaps we need to consider how God could be speaking to us through these means.

Another recent dream of significance happened during some challenging times leading up to writing this book. One morning I woke up and my wife could tell I was troubled. Over morning coffee, I explained that I had a dream wherein someone died. She asked who died in the dream, so I told her some doctors in my dream told me I only had twelve hours to live. However, I knew what the doctors were telling me was wrong, and that it was not me who would be dead in a few hours. In the dream I repeatedly told the doctors they were confused and that it was not me who was going to die. I told my wife that I hoped none of it was true because my sense was that it was about someone close to me. After telling her this we left for church. Shortly after we sat down at church, I got a phone call from my brother Brian with a message that our thirty-year-old brother Jon suddenly died while on a boat, water skiing with close friends. Unfortunately, my dream was warning me of a death that was close enough to me that it was, in a sense, part of me.

I have had other vivid dreams in my life that foretold events, but most seem to be dreams warning that something is going on. Fortunately, these dreams are infrequent, but they are very different than the stream of dreams that I get most nights. The dreams that go beyond the random nature of our own minds because of the vivid nature of the dreams and the messages attached to them need to be weighed more carefully.

We all put up walls and barriers that keep us from experiencing a full relationship with the Father, the Son, and the Spirit. The more we can allow ourselves to have hearts like those of a child—with attentive ears and open eyes—the more likely we are to experience His presence. God gives us evidence of his presence in various ways, yet because of our walls, do we sometimes make him small and even obsolete? Why do we limit a limitless God?

Questions to Ponder

What one concept or statement in this chapter struck you the most? Explain why.

What boundaries do you believe you have created in your belief systems of God that limit him, and thus limit your faith?

What boundaries do you feel your current "religious" beliefs have placed on God?

What are the potential consequences of your false boundaries?

Is there an area of your life in which you feel spiritual strongholds persist enough to keep you out of God's desires for you?

CHAPTER 4

Underestimating God

I N THE FIRST CHAPTER, we focused on faith and how most of us lack "the faith of a child." Remember, Jesus suggested it is necessary to have an unhindered, childlike level of faith to enter the kingdom of God:

> *"Jesus said, 'I tell you the truth, anyone who will not receive the kingdom of God like a little child will never enter it.'" Luke 18:17*

In another verse Jesus also says we won't be able to see the activity of the kingdom of God unless we are "born again":

> *"In reply Jesus declared, 'I tell you the truth, no one can see the kingdom of God unless he is born again.'" John 3:3*

If you are not familiar with the idea of being born again, in the Christian faith being born again means to have received the Holy Spirit as a result of knowing sin has separated us from God and, in order to mend this separation, requesting a relationship with Jesus, the Father and the Holy Spirit. Through Jesus the doors of heaven become open to us and through the Spirit within we have the potential to see and sense God's kingdom at work around us.

When we see the world around us only through our adult eyes, we often miss witnessing the kingdom of God at work because we lack the positive expectancy that God is present and actively at work all around us. We all know that when we are born we begin the life of a child. Likewise, when we are born again through the indwelling of the Holy Spirit, we begin the life of a spiritually adopted child of God. We become kids of the King, and as his children we can expect good things from our Father who loves us.

> *And so, we know and rely on the love God has for us. God*
> *is love. Whoever lives in love lives in God, and God in him.*
> *1 John 4:16*

Because "God is Love," we can expect love from him. If his Spirit indwells us, we are also expected to manifest his love to others.

In the second chapter, we looked at gratitude because gratitude is an expression of the faith contained within our hearts. When we grumble and complain, we essentially say God is not at work and does not care. On the other hand, if we have the faith of a child, we will express gratitude because we expect and believe God is at work doing good. We trust in his presence and his desire to make things right. We have gratitude because we have faith that Abba (Daddy) is at work, even when His presence is not immediately sensed, or the results of his behind-the-scenes work is not evident to our eyes yet:

> *"Now faith is being sure of what we hope for and certain of*
> *what we do not see." Heb. 11:1*

In the previous chapter, we concentrated on potential ways that we put up walls, which in turn create the limiting box of faith that we live within. Essentially, we put up self-made walls and barriers to who God really is, making God into our own image. These walls get erected for many reasons, but nonetheless all of our walls (and therefore our image of God) are narrow and restrictive as compared to God's unlimited power.

To one degree or another, we all operate on some form of self-induced falsehoods. In the end, most of us create in our own minds a God whom we are comfortable with. If the walls we have built around our image of God are incorrect, they may hold us captive to false beliefs that hinder our relationship with him and interfere with a correct view of reality. As a vivid reminder, the religious leaders of Jesus' day knew more about the prophecies of Christ than anyone, yet they failed to see who he really was because they were trapped by false beliefs that blinded them to God's perspective of reality. Jesus did not fit into the box they had made for the Messiah. No doubt in their minds, the Messiah would have been in full agreement with them; after all, they were God's elect and the most educated in God's word. Jesus was not pleased with their stubborn hearts (walls), and he let them know it! He said:

> *"Woe to you, teachers of the law and Pharisees, you hypocrites! You are like whitewashed tombs, which look beautiful on the outside but on the inside are full of dead men's bones and everything unclean. In the same way, on the outside you appear to people as righteous but on the inside you are full of hypocrisy and wickedness." Matt. 23:27–28*

Seeking Reality

In this chapter, we are going to get a little crazy and somewhat speculative. It is likely that even with our wildest imaginations at work, we will fall far short of the reality of who God is. It is a fact for all of us that we understand little about the spiritual world that surrounds us. We have an infant-like understanding of the spiritual realm. Truthfully, all of us are in need of deconstructing our walls to see God more accurately. For most of us, the image of God we have created has been "humanized" so that we are comfortable with our concepts and relational beliefs of who God is. We make him small enough to maintain our own comfort levels. In the end, walls limit our faith, reduce our hope, and steal our gratitude. Walls cause us to live short of the joy and freedom that God intends for us to have on earth.

Scripture expresses that it is God's will for us to experience fullness of life (shalom) on earth, *as it will be in heaven*, and this can only happen when his Holy Spirit indwells us. In conjunction with the power of the Holy Spirit, the kingdom takes up residence in our hearts and God can begin to transform our hearts and minds. If truth is God's perspective of reality, we are more likely to learn his perspective when his Spirit resides in us and directs our hearts and minds toward seeing things through his eyes. Part of the Lord's prayer is that we request God's perspective of reality so that we experience on earth, just as it would be as if we lived in heaven:

> *"... your kingdom come, your will be done on earth (and in our lives) as it is in heaven." Matt. 6:10*

Science and Man's Wisdom

Every culture has within it lies from the devil intended to distract us from knowing the one true God. In Western civilization, we cannot begin to engage in tearing down walls without looking at the distortions, "in the name of science," that have been drilled into most of us. In one sense, it will be hard to see God for who he is without breaking down the false walls of Naturalism and Darwinian Evolution. Being a person with a science background, I find science to be rather fascinating because it is a process of discovery. Almost all early science came from exploratory people who had a belief in God, so the exploration of the world and all that is in it was a process of discovering what God had created so we might better understand him. Unfortunately, certain narrow and restrictive views of science today have as their foundation a perspective that excludes God as an answer to anything. Too much of today's academia is focused on trying to figure out ways to say God had nothing to do with all the precision and creativity that is inherent in every living thing:

> *"God made the wild animals according to their kinds, the livestock according to their kinds, and all the creatures that move along the ground according to their kinds. And God saw that it was good." Genesis 1:25*

Realistically, we cannot put an accurate number to all the processes that would need to take place for life to exist in the simplest of forms. Depending on where we want to draw the line, there are billions of unique forms of life created with the precision to function in diverse habitats around the globe. The more scientific knowledge we have, the more obvious it becomes that Darwinian

Evolution is only a sad means of trying to rule out God. Evolution (Naturalism) is the hope the godless have in saying, "God does not exist." They have not only erected walls around their boxes of faith, but they have also put a roof on the box so as to shut God out completely. The greatest source of information about the universe is the Creator himself; when we shut him out, the only source of information we have left is the knowledge of the secular world of men, which is routinely flawed:

> *"For the foolishness of God is wiser than man's wisdom,*
> *and the weakness of God is stronger than man's strength."*
> *1 Cor. 1:25*

In a godless state of being, our box of reality is contained within our finite mind, and we effectively shut out the mind of the infinite. No doubt a prideful, egocentric, human is a sad sight to God. Too often, egos in the arena of science and academia become falsely elevated and perverted. The largest danger for those in this situation is when their words and actions lead others astray. Leading others away from God is likely to be met with God's righteous judgement either in this life or the life to come. To be sure, a spiritual battle surrounds this issue, and there is often an underlying intent to draw us away from God. There is a Spirit of the Antichrist whose full intention is to blind humans to the pathway to God. As foolish as a godless evolution of life is, it has been used effectively to blind many from seeing the truth, and it has become a weapon of the "prince of this world," so named by John in this verse:

> *"The prince of this world now stands condemned." John*
> *16:11*

One of Satan's biggest lies is making misguided science an alternative to God by putting hope in the fairytale of Darwinian Evolution which essentially says all of life was merely a giant and continuous series of random events. The apostle Paul warns us that we must be careful of any theories or philosophies whose underlying premise removes God as a possible answer:

> *"Where is the wise man? Where is the scholar? Where is the philosopher of this age? Has not God made foolish the wisdom of the world?" 1 Cor. 1:20*

Evolution

Darwinian Evolution at best is a wall that says, "God isn't and God didn't." Evolution at its worst is the roof placed on our self-made boxes that says, "God does not exist." There is no doubt that God designed many features within his creation that operate at very deep levels, and we will continue to understand them better because of the curiosity of scientifically gifted minds. Oddly, discoveries relating to the precision in all life forms are too often written off with the absurd notion that randomness keeps making things perfect. Interestingly, egocentric, self-absorbed, and supposedly intelligent people can be the most closed off people to the abundant realities God puts right before our eyes.

The most advanced technological systems ever created were not made by man, nor by total random chance; rather, they exist and survive because they were specifically designed to do so. God created many things that helps his creation of all living things survive, and some forms of adaptations exist, but this also was a created feature, not randomness. The point is, many of us have fallen into the ideas of godless evolutionary theories and/or philosophies of naturalism, and we have erected at least a partial wall of disbelief in God because of it. To be sure, God's perspective of reality is nowhere close to where a Darwinian Evolutionist stands:

> *"As it is written: 'God gave them a spirit of stupor, eyes so that they could not see.'" Rom. 11:8*

God's Handiwork

The exploration of science has revealed more and more about our Creator. When the Bible was written, the world did not revolve around the scientific knowledge we have today. Science has revealed, and will continue to reveal, the creative genius behind all of life. The more we learn about the intricacies of life, the more it should illuminate God and help us recognize that he is far beyond our wildest imagination. Since it is our mortal tendency to humanize God, and thus make him smaller, weaker, and less ingenious, the more likely we are to say, "God couldn't do all this." The incredibly odd part of this is rather than admitting that this Creator is so far beyond our comprehension, we actually fall back on the absolute impossibility that random accidents caused it. It would be a similar analogy to have an alien visit our planet and observe all the art and architecture on earth and say that they don't know how all the colors and structures came to be, but somehow over billions of years beauty and structural precision just happened.

God is well aware of everything we learn through science because he made it all. If we believe in a God who participates in our lives, then we have to consider that God may have given some men and women of science the ideas that led to their discoveries. Wouldn't a loving God lead us on paths of discovery to potentially help his creation flourish on this planet, and to increasingly reveal himself to us through these discoveries? For instance, Einstein (long before it was provable) came up with the theory that if we could travel at the speed of light, we would cease to age. In time, science has shown this to be true through subatomic particles, which travel at or beyond the speed of light and they cease having any form of a half-life, or any detectable rate of decay. When we consider the Biblical idea of eternal life and consider the statement, "God is light," then perhaps this statement holds a deeper meaning than most of us assume. Because God is spirit (not physical), then perhaps a being existing in some form of light energy would be eternal. Possibly God gave Einstein these thoughts to expose a new reality, something outside of the physical realities of our human lives:

> "Through him all things were made; without him nothing was made that has been made. In him was life, and that life was the light of men. The light shines in the darkness, but the darkness has not understood it." John 1:3–5

"This is the message we have heard from him and declare to you: God is light; in him there is no darkness at all."
1 John 1:5

Many scientists also believe in the "Big Bang" theory as the inaugural occurrence for all of life. The problem this theory presents is that there has to be a beginning—everything physical has to have a "first cause." If there was a Big Bang, then there had to be a mass big enough to account for every star and planet in the universe. This mass then had to explode and shoot off massive objects that we call our suns and planets, which then formed into galaxies with millions of stars. However, it is evident that the galaxies are hung throughout space in spectacular form and fashion, not is disarray after an explosion. Also, somehow after the "Big Bang," our particular sun attracted perfectly round planets as a result of this explosion and the planets adjusted themselves into perfect orbit around our sun. To the best of our knowledge, if we drop any one of these planets from our solar system, then everything falls apart; and if our sun was not just the perfect size, all of it would fail. Then, this lifeless plant Earth somehow had to have an environment that allowed for development of proteins from all kinds of other perfectly balanced chemicals, which in turn assembled to form a cell. But for a cell to exist, complex working units within the cell (organelles) are needed for it to exist and function. These organelles are essentially like the organs in our bodies, such as kidneys, hearts, livers, and a neurochemical brain. These microscopic organelles had to first form themselves and then learn to function together to keep this cell alive. If this was not enough of a stretch of the imagination, this first cell then had to figure out a way to divide to make baby cells.

The absurdity of evolutionary theory goes on and on. Man is a puny little speck in a massive universe, and we too often think we have things totally figured out. God is either laughing or crying over our absurd conclusions of life forming and developing without him. Fortunately, God is very aware there is a spirit of delusion behind all of this, and I believe he shows us a certain degree of grace in our ignorance.

"But every spirit that does not acknowledge Jesus is not from God. This is the spirit of the antichrist, which you have heard is coming and even now is already in the world." 1 John 4:3

The Designer

The many complexities we learn about life forms should not point us away from God but toward him. If we believe species have adapted, it is because it was built into them to have this potential. To be sure, fish did not evolve into mammals, nor did insects eventually become fish, etc. Species were created in wholeness with some abilities to adapt, but not change species. God designed some potential to change but only through small modifications within specifically created lifeforms. Consider that God created the beautifully colored zebra; although related to horses, it cannot successfully breed with horses, and this preserves the integrity of the created artwork of the zebra. The fabulous colors of the striped tiger can't be altered by breeding with the amazing spotted leopard. Although they are both big cats, they can't breed successfully. Again, the two are intentionally kept separate to preserve their original design and artwork. There are all kinds of examples like this in nature and they are by design. God is very intentional, and like any artist he wants many of his "works of art" to remain unaltered so we can enjoy and marvel at his creative talents. Consider that God creates certain barriers by design to preserve certain elements of his creation while others he purposefully leaves open so his garden of life grows in uniquely beautiful ways.

When someone says they discovered a completely new species, you might consider the possibility that it was not under our noses all the time. Rather than jumping to the sole conclusion that this new lifeform had simply not been noticed before, perhaps we might speculate that our incredibly creative God put it in our path in a completed state. Might he do this to draw our attention to him? Maybe he tests us to see if we are observant and operating with the wonderment of a child. Why would we assume that the God of all creation simply stopped creating? When we build a wall that says God didn't create, or that he only created once and then quit, then maybe this wall doesn't let us see that he is present, still creating, and showing off a bit. Maybe he puts us all to the test and says, "What do you believe, some of the godless beliefs of science and evolution, or in me?" Why do we put limits on a limitless God?

> *"By faith we understand that the universe was formed at God's command, so that what is seen was not made out of what was visible." Heb. 11:3*

> *"He is before all things, and in him all things hold together." Col 1:16*

Our Internal Prison

A critical point in this discussion that we need to be aware of is that our hearts and our minds can become our own self-imprisonment. The more we exist within our own minds, the deeper our prisons become. Freedom from this internal imprisonment is only found through the indwelling of the Holy Spirit. The more we allow the Spirit to act and speak through us, the fuller life becomes. The Spirit brings knowledge and a peace that surpasses our understanding. It surpasses our understanding because it does not come from within, but from an outside source we call God. We were created in his image to host his Spirit, but when we shut this down, we imprison ourselves to a very limited existence. Because we were created as "spiritually wired" beings, this gives us the ability to host the Holy Spirit. However, this same spiritual wiring leaves room for spiritual influence from Satan, the Prince of this world:

> *"Jesus said, 'The thief (Satan) comes only to steal and kill and destroy; I have come that they may have life, and have it to the full.'" John 10:10*

Things to Consider

Consider some of these brief aspects of God:

- He is spirit, not physical in nature like everything else we are familiar with on this earth.

- He is a spirit being that has the capability of creating physical things out of nothing.

- He created the universe, potentially through something like a big bang. However, rather than this explosion creating a mass of flying debris through the heavens, it created planets, suns, and spectacular galaxies. This massive explosion (if that was the initial creation occurrence) created symmetry rather than randomness.

- He created every cell type within every microbe, insect, reptile, bird, mammal, fish, and plant.

- He created the internal chemistry of every life form with the precision necessary to exist.

- Beavers build dams, monarch butterflies fly to Mexico every year, and bees pollinate flowers. They do this not because they know what they are doing, but the creator specifically and individually designed them to enable balance and harmony on his planet Earth.

- Did you know that the universe was not just set in place, but that it is a living organism of sorts? Yes, science through the use of massive telescopes seems rather certain that new suns are actually being birthed in birthing chambers of some kind. Did he make those too, or did it just happen?

The deeper we explore, the more it should lead us towards God, but when we truly explore who he is and what he is capable of, our minds tend to shut down because he is *too* much for us. We cannot truly grasp the enormity of who God is. We either simplify him in the boxes we create, or we shut him out and look for alternative explanations for the cause and meaning of life. We are dumb sheep, either dumb sheep that follow him, or dumb sheep that ignore him and shut him out.

In the end, God created a path for us to have an eternal existence with him in a Kingdom he designed for us to be part of, both now and in the life to come. God keeps the door to relationship with him open and simple, because we need simple. God tells us that if we truly seek him, through his son Jesus, that he will answer our call. God has made a way out of the darkness and into his light:

> *"Jesus said: 'Ask and it will be given to you; seek and you will find; knock and the door will be opened to you. For everyone who asks receives; he who seeks finds; and to him who knocks, the door will be opened.'" Matt. 7:7*

> *"Jesus answered, 'I am the way and the truth and the life. No one comes to the Father except through me.'" John 14:6*

> *"Yet to all who received him, to those who believed in his name, he gave the right to become children of God—children born not of natural descent, nor of human decision or a husband's will, but born of God." John 1:12–13*

Life Story

Perhaps the fact that God is capable of being intimately part of your life and mine, while also having unique and individual relationships with millions of people on the planet at the same time, should open our minds to the fact that God is unlike anybody or anything we can comprehend. Sometimes God communicates through subtle, day-to-day ways, but God can also reveal himself to us through unique circumstances that seem to be planned in detail and set in motion decades or years beforehand.

God's involvement in my life has been personal and full of grace, like a loving father to his child. My experience within this relationship is not fully unique from the standpoint that God involves himself in very personal ways in the lives of all who invite him in. As Kids of the King, we all have equal access to our Father.

When I was twenty-four years old, I traveled from Michigan to Arizona to meet with a doctor about an idea I had about a total health facility. I made a model of the building that would illustrate this concept and traveled solo across the country in my car to share the idea with this prominent individual. Even when I'm alone, I must say that I never really feel like I am by myself because I sense God is present and listening. Especially on a long journey like this, my mind becomes filled with all kinds of thoughts. Some of these thoughts I bring to his attention, as if we are having a conversation about them. Sometimes funny "human behavioral" thoughts and observations come up and I joke with God about these things as well. I believe that too often we see God as a serious character who does not laugh and only occasionally shares a smile. But this is not an accurate understanding of who God is?

After my meeting in Phoenix, I headed out to return to my home in Michigan and on the way back I toured the rim of the Grand Canyon. Photography has been a hobby of mine, and the Grand Canyon is an amazing place to photograph. Individual rain clouds were rolling past all day, and some dropped scattered light rain as they passed through. When I was near the edge of the canyon, with a metal guard rail in front of me, one of the passing clouds released a bolt of lightning. The main bolt split up into multiple smaller bolts. One of the smaller offshoots of lightning went through me on the way to the metal guard rail in front of me. The surge of electrical current passing through me caused all my muscles to contract at once. Standing some distance behind me was an old Arizona cowboy who exclaimed, "OOOEEE, this boy got hit!"

After the cowboy made sure I was alright, he went on to tell me that he had been hit by lightning while riding a horse on his ranch in Arizona. He asked me if I could hear it crackle in my head and if I could taste it. My answer was, "Yes!" Fortunately, I was hit by an offshoot of the main bolt, otherwise I doubt I would be writing about it today. After a short recovery, I walked back to my car and drove off, reeling from the experience. As I drove away, I was talking to God again, saying, "Hey God, you would think that with all these passing rain clouds you would at least give me a rainbow to photograph, rather than being hit by a bolt of lightning."

The next scenic turnoff was only a short distance away, so I pulled in and walked over toward an edge. As I neared the edge of the canyon, I looked down through a ravine that extended all the way down to the bottom of the canyon. To my delight there was not one, but three rainbows, all stacked one on top of the other. The rainbows went from one wall of the ravine to the other, but they were only visible from my vantage point over the edge of the canyon, not from the road that rimmed the canyon. Thrilled by God's almost instant answer to my request for a rainbow, I turned around and there was only one other lone woman nearby. I proceeded to share with her how I was hit by lightning just minutes ago, and how I conversed with God about the lack of rainbows despite the periodic rain showers. This may sound odd, but there was something different about her presence there, and in hindsight I don't recall ever seeing another vehicle when I pulled into this area. Part of me wonders about this strategically placed woman. Perhaps it was an angel getting a kick out of my story and my surprise of God's provision. Probably not, but I am not ruling it out.

Additionally, as I have mentioned previously, God has often made himself known to me through the number three. The fact that I was alive and feeling well after being hit by lightning, followed by the provision of not one but *three* rainbows after my childlike request, was a clear sign, in my perspective, that God was traveling with me and watching over me. Obviously, these things could be total coincidences, but because of how God personally communicates with me, I doubt that very much. Besides, why would I want to limit a limitless God because of my own self-doubt?

Questions to Consider

Was there one concept or statement in this chapter that struck you the most? Explain why.

Why do you suppose science tries to exclude God?

In your estimation could the press for embracing Darwinian Evolution as the sole explanation of life be part of a spiritual battle?

If there is a Satan, would he have an interest in the Darwinian Evolution discussion? Why?

Life's Spiritual Influences

Sensing the Spirit Realm

THE BEST-SELLING MOVIES OF all time have been those based on the Marvel cartoon series. In these movies both human and immortal characters fight evil to preserve the lives of the innocent, and good nearly always prevails. Star Wars is another series that people attended in droves to watch the power of the Force overcome the evil of the Dark Side. Yes, the special effects in these movies are superb, but I believe there is something written on the heart of humans that knows, almost without question, that there is good and evil at work around us. Perhaps we are drawn to these movies not because they are total fantasy but because they represent a subconscious, spiritual understanding that good and evil forces exist, and that they are in combat around us. Perhaps you are even involved in this combat at times, whether you are aware of it or not.

The spirit realm is not visible to us, but most people believe it exists in one form or another. We believe in the spiritual world because we can sense it and sometimes witness supernatural elements of it. Most of us in the "civilized" Western culture believe angels exist, but many are afraid to admit, or in denial, that demons exist. There are areas of the world where demonic possession and Satan's overt activity are much more common. Consider why in Western civilization demonic possession is less visible than it is in third world countries. Perhaps this is because much of Western culture has stopped believing Satan exists, and displays of outright possession would alert the unaware to the presence of demons. Satan would rather we don't believe in him so that he can manipulate us in more subtle ways without alerting us to his presence.

Marvel, Star Wars, and endless Hollywood productions portray good and evil, not because it doesn't exist, but because it does. These movies resonate with a deeper knowing in our beings. If in fact the spirit world exists, it exists in a different dimension than we live in. In all likelihood, the spirit world sees us very clearly, but our human eyes are unable to see into their realm the same way. Potentially, depending on our environments, there are spiritual forces all around us. Good and Evil have distinct personalities because there are persons, or spiritual beings, behind their activity. Once we learn more about their personalities, it might change the way we look at life and the events of the world. More to come on this subject in the chapters to follow.

Spiritual DNA

Because we were created in God's image, who is a spiritual being, we have built within us the capacity to receive spiritual things. In fact, if you are a born-again believer, you have the Spirit of God indwelling you. In essence, humans have some capabilities of interacting with the spiritual realm, whether we are aware of a spiritual presence or not. Most likely, prior to the spiritual separation between God and mankind that was caused by the sin of Adam and Eve, our capacities for spiritual interactions were greatly magnified from what we experience as God's creation today. Still, there are parts of us that can receive and interact with the spirit realm. In a sense, we have "spiritual DNA" imprinted into us that enables us to interact with the spiritual realm. Because God is Spirit and we are created in his image, we too have spiritual leanings:

> *"So God created man in his own image, in the image of God he created him . . . " Gen. 1:27*

Let's put some of this into basic concepts. God is a personal being and he is spiritual in nature. Humans were created to be in relationship with God and we have a heart, mind, and soul/spirit capable of being directed by the Holy Spirit:

> *"Jesus replied: "'Love the Lord your God with all your heart and with all your soul and with all your mind.'" Matt. 22:37*

The spiritual nature of mankind is a commonality, a shared attribute, between mankind and the Creator. However, although we have this spiritual component, the battle for our souls between the spiritual forces of good and evil begins in our minds:

> *"To the pure, all things are pure, but to those who are corrupted and do not believe, nothing is pure. In fact, both their minds and consciences are corrupted." Titus 1:15*

Thoughts from both sides come into our minds, and what we choose to do with these thoughts, (by our own will and by our decisions regarding the voices we follow) often regulates our path in life. This path may be toward God or away from him, depending on our willful choices and the degree of relationship we have with God. Ultimately, a heart-felt and voluntary request for the entry of the Holy Spirit, through Jesus Christ, is the means to an internal, transforming presence of God:

> *"Jesus said: "'But I tell you the truth: It is for your good that I am going away. Unless I go away, the Counselor (Holy Spirit) will not come to you; but if I go, I will send him to you. When he comes, he will convict the world of guilt in regard to sin and righteousness and judgment: in regard to sin, because men do not believe in me; in regard to righteousness, because I am going to the Father, where you can see me no longer; and in regard to judgment, because the prince of this world now stands condemned.'" John 16:7-11*

Satan's Personhood

As we walk through this life, we are likely not walking it alone. As Jesus acknowledged, there is a prince of this world. He only refers to him as a prince because he controls or runs much of it, but not all of it. This prince is Satan, and this being has a distinct personality. If we can recognize his personality, we can begin to identify his work. At this point in history, his work has a primary purpose and that is to lead people astray from knowing God through Jesus Christ. In the Bible he is referred to as the "Spirit of the Antichrist," because he is *anti* (the antithesis) to Christ.

The world is full of falsehoods that lead people astray. When you want to observe Satan's work, simply observe the things that are purposefully designed to lead humans away from a personal relationship with God and his Son, Jesus. Keep in mind that Satan is not always in-your-face obvious. Satan is a clever deceiver, and he likely knows how to play most of us like a fiddle. Because we have used the concept of falsehood in the discussion of building walls that limit God, a definition of falsehood for the purposes of this discussion is anything we believe and orient our lives around that is not in conjunction with God's view of reality. All of Satan's activities are designed as falsehoods to build walls between us and God:

> *" Jesus said: 'You belong to your father, the devil, and you want to carry out your father's desire. He was a murderer from the beginning, not holding to the truth, for there is no truth in him. When he lies, he speaks his native language, for he is a liar and the father of lies.'" John 8:44*

> *"Many deceivers, who do not acknowledge Jesus Christ as coming in the flesh, have gone out into the world. Any such person is the deceiver and the antichrist." 2 John 7*

> *"But every spirit that does not acknowledge Jesus is not from God. This is the spirit of the antichrist, which you have heard is coming and even now is already in the world." 1 John 4:3*

Satan's Origin

Let's pull back a moment and look at what Scripture says about this spiritual realm. First, Satan was not always Satan. Satan originally was a powerful angel. This angel developed or had some serious dysfunction, but it is not clear as to just what that was. There was something lacking in him. Because God is love, perhaps he was missing this capacity? Maybe pride and ego made him believe he was more than he was. We really do not know with certainty his troubles. But here is something we do know:

> *"And there was war in heaven. Michael and his angels fought against the dragon, and the dragon and his angels fought back. But he was not strong enough, and they lost their place in heaven. The great dragon was hurled down— that ancient serpent called the devil, or Satan, who leads the whole world astray. He was hurled to the earth, and his angels with him." Rev. 12:7–9*

As far as we know angels are created beings, just as we are. The purpose of angels is to serve God in various capacities and to come alongside those people called by God:

> *"Are not all angels ministering spirits sent to serve those who will inherit salvation?" Heb. 1:14*

We also know that Satan thought very highly of himself and felt he could ascend to heaven and overthrow God. Notice Satan's "I wills" in the following passage:

> *"You said in your heart, 'I will ascend to heaven; I will raise my throne above the stars of God; I will sit enthroned on the mount of assembly, on the utmost heights of the sacred mountain. I will ascend above the tops of the clouds; I will make myself like the Most High.'" Is. 14:13–14*

Satan has an incredible power to influence, leading even angels astray. It is a biblical understanding that one-third of the angels followed Satan in an attempt to overthrow God's kingdom. Just what this means is hard to know, but it is clear that Satan and these angels were cast down to earth. In their fallen state, they are considered demonic beings and no longer hold on to their angelic beauty, neither in their physical state nor in their personality. When cast down to earth, Satan set out to destroy the bond between God and his newly formed crown of creation, humankind. This is the story of the garden of Eden (Genesis 3), when Adam and Eve were deceived by this cunning being. From this time forth, Satan has continued to try to separate mankind from their creator. SInce Satan hates God, he also hates his image bearers. Furthermore, God's plan for mankind was to be in perfect relationship with him, but our sin creates a separation between us and God. Sin can create a barrier between God and us for an eternity, and this is Satan's desire. The personality behind evil is strategic and deceptive; it can even appear as an angel of light in order to deceive us. Satan has a consistently destructive game-plan, so it is important for us to try and detect and know his personality:

> *"The thief comes only to steal and kill and destroy." John 10:10*

> *"And no wonder, for Satan himself masquerades as an angel of light." 2 Cor. 11:14*

How Many Angels and Demons Exist?

When we wonder about the potential influence that angelic and demonic forces may have on earth, it would be helpful for us to conceptualize it in numbers. When considering the potential spiritual influence in our world, we first need to realize that God is omnipresent, but Satan is not. Therefore, God can be everywhere at the same time. On the other hand, Satan is a single character who relies on his demonic troops to carry out his plans in locations around the globe. When we hear that one-third of the angels fell and potentially all became demons, we really need to have some concept of just how many angels fell to have an idea of their worldwide influence. This is not for us to know with any certainty, but we may be able to get a glimpse from these numbers in the book of Revelation when John saw the heavenly realm:

> *"Then I looked and heard the voice of many angels, numbering thousands upon thousands, and ten thousand times ten thousand. They encircled the throne and the living creatures and the elders." Rev. 5:11*

Again, if these numbers are correct, then ten thousand multiplied by ten thousand would be one hundred million angels present during John's "vision" into God's kingdom. Furthermore, if we believe there are guardian angels for each believer on the planet (which I do not feel is acknowledged in Scripture) then we are potentially talking about billions of angelic beings because there are an estimated 2.2 billion people who "claim" the Christian faith. There is no way for us to know with any certainty, but if one third of the angels fell with Satan, then how many millions are roaming about planet earth? The only reason this really comes into the discussion is so that we at least have an awareness of the possibility that Satan and the demons could be abundant enough to potentially whisper into many of our ears, the ears of false teachers, world leaders, cult members, gang members, etc. The dark side of the spirit realm engages in a vast network of schemes to create death, despair, and destruction, while simultaneously undermining the salvation given through Jesus Christ. Satan's troops are likely to be plentiful, and thus evil is observable and prevalent around the globe.

Another thought to consider: why does the Spirit of the Antichrist have his focus on Christ? Well, if Jesus is who he claimed to be, then a relationship with Jesus is the entrance to eternal life. Because of Satan's hatred for God and his disdain for God's image bearers, he desperately wants to lead as many astray as he can before his end comes. Satan is aware that Jesus professed:

> *"I am the way and the truth and the life. No one comes to the Father except through me." John 14:6*

When we look at the potential for demonic influence in our individual lives, we should not downplay the possibility for direct contact with personalities of evil. It seems as though angels are plentiful, yet potentially one-third of them now exist as demonic entities on earth. Knowing that a primary purpose of these forces is to keep us from the truth of God, we must consider that some of our own walls that isolate us from God may not be merely creations of our environment or our minds, but clever plans devised by God's foes in order to keep God's creation from experiencing unity with him. Jesus seemed to be aware enough of these forces to request that God protect his followers once he ascended from earth because he would no longer be there to protect them:

> *"My prayer is not that you take them out of the world but that you protect them from the evil one." John 17:15*

Distinct Personalities

The persons of God and Satan have very different personalities. God is a God of love who wants only good for his creation. Satan would like to obliterate life and take people away from God before they can come to a saving faith, a faith that will carry them into an eternal destiny in God's kingdom. The disciple Peter believes that:

> *"Your enemy the devil prowls around like a roaring lion looking for someone to devour." 1 Peter 5:8*

The Church has always taught that Satan is a personal being and a supremely intelligent spirit who has rebelled against God, and is an enemy of humankind.

Life Story

When you enter a relationship with Jesus, the process of spiritual rebirth and progressive redevelopment of who you are begins. There was a time in my mid-thirties when I came to understand that the gift of tongues can be a way the Holy Spirit speaks through us directly. I don't believe Satan likes to see someone genuinely empowered by the Holy Spirit in this way.

About the time I was twenty years old, my mother had spoken in tongues. This especially intrigued me because she did so during trials in her life, when she especially needed the peace and reassurance of Jesus Christ. I believed in the gift, but I had not personally manifested it. As I learned more about the Holy Spirit and the gift of tongues, I decided to request it from Jesus, the Father, and the Holy Spirit.

My story is very similar to that of many people who have encountered Satan and/or his demon followers. When I was seeking this gift of tongues, I experienced three back-to-back events that I believe were the demonic world's way of trying to scare me off my path. The first of these events was a dream, but it was not fully a dream. As I was lying in bed, part of this event was very real, almost as if I was partially in a dream and partially awake and aware of my surroundings. To this day it is hard to know where the dream began and ended and when the real person/demon became present.

This is what happened. Past the foot of the bed and well off in the distance was a clown-like character with a multi-colored hat that had three triangular extensions, each extension coming off the sides of the hat. It was kind of like a stocking hat with three rather than one extension. I knew the entity was evil and of Satan, but he was disguised as a silly clown. I don't remember exactly what I said, but I mocked him. As soon as I mocked him, the hat started to spin like the blades on a fan, and it came directly at me with a blur of rotating colors. As it drew near to me, I sat up in bed and the object stopped about one foot in front of my face. Before my eyes the hat disappeared and only the face of the demon was there. It was a hairy, red-eyed face that would scare the crap out of anyone. At this moment I felt fully awake, and then it vanished before my eyes. It still freaks me out all these years later.

The next day was Sunday, so my wife and I went to church. As we were sitting in the pews and our pastor was speaking, I saw an image of myself getting up, walking to the aisle, and pointing a rifle down the aisle toward the pastor. Like the clown-demon, this vision also left as quickly as it came. I'm sure it all happened in my mind within just seconds, but it was another encounter with evil that felt real and tangible. I loved my pastor, and this vision struck my heart with fear and grief.

The next day, I was coming out of my office and felt an oppressive spirit upon me that had been lingering with me since the demon-dream a few days before. Because Scripture says that as believers we can rebuke the Devil in the name of Jesus Christ and he will flee from us, I verbally rebuked the evil spirit of oppression that seemed to surround me. I rebuked it in the name of Jesus Christ. Yet, I still did not feel like it had left me. The oppression was still there. As I sat in my truck I decided to try another tactic, something that I had never done before. I said, "Angels of God, if whatever evil is present does not heed my rebuke in the name of Jesus Christ, I give you authority to dash them to pieces." Immediately, it was as if someone turned on a bright light. The air about me seemed to illuminate an elevated form of light and the oppressive energy that was around me disappeared in an instant.

My story is not unique. It is not uncommon when someone has a relationship with Jesus that spiritual forces of evil may try to thwart their faith-driven life by fearful events or difficult life circumstances. Satan knows he is going to lose his battle against God, and he knows his time is limited. Because of this, Satan is trying to bring as many people with him as he can. Satan will try to lead you on any path that steers you away from a deeper relationship with Christ. If Satan is trying to interfere with your life, it is because you're going in the direction that he does not want you to, which is towards God and his desires/purposes. Knowing this should increase our resolve to stay the course rather than back down when we feel or experience evil spiritual influences. For he who is in us is greater than he who is in the world. We are more than conquerors who ultimately have no one or nothing to fear:

> *"No, in all these things we are more than conquerors through him who loved us. For I am convinced that neither death nor life, neither angels nor demons, neither the present nor the future, nor any powers, neither height nor depth, nor anything else in all creation, will be able to separate us from the love of God that is in Christ Jesus our Lord." Romans 8:37–38*

Two Realms

Let's ponder how the spirit world and our world co-exist. It is believed by many that there is some type of interwoven union on this earth between mankind and spiritual beings, in essence there is an overlap of two different realms of existence. One realm is physical in nature and the other is spiritual:

> *"Once you were dead because of your disobedience and your many sins. You used to live in sin, just like the rest of the world, obeying the devil—the commander of the powers in the unseen world." Ephesians 2:1*

For descriptive purposes, we will call the separation between these two realms a "fabric" of sorts. This fabric acts like a curtain or veil that separates us visually but not physically. Just what this fabric is made up of, or caused by, is not clear from our human vantage point. The spirit world and our physical world intermingle. Angelic encounters have been recorded in the Bible and in other writings throughout history. Obvious demonic possessions are still present in the world. Things we call ghosts, phantoms, or apparitions are potentially glimpses into this existing spiritual realm. There are those who worship Satan and the occult who will very directly tell you they have contact with demonic beings. It appears that a disadvantage of being in the human, physical realm is that we can't see the spiritual realm, but the reciprocal is most likely not true. Angels and demons probably can see our physical world at all times. The question that will never be answered on this side of heaven is just how much spiritual involvement there is in each one of our lives. The level of demonic spiritual influence in our lives is likely dependent on how vulnerable we leave ourselves because of our ignorance and/or our false beliefs. Again, it is important to keep in mind that since Satan is not omnipresent, and thus cannot oversee or control all things on his own, most of his work is done by his demons who are unified by Satan's vision of destruction.

Another fascinating observation is that it is hard to say for certain whether the biblical sightings of angels were due to the angels taking on physical form, or if God allows for the eyes of people to be opened to see into the spiritual realm for a moment in time. Take for example the time when an army surrounded the prophet

Elisha. Elisha was confident in God's angelic protection, but his servant was understandably in a panic for his very life:

> *"Elisha told his servant, 'Don't be afraid,' the prophet answered. 'Those who are with us are more than those who are with them. Then Elisha prayed, 'O LORD, open his eyes so he may see.' Then the LORD opened the servant's eyes, and he looked and saw the hills full of horses and chariots of fire all around Elisha." 2 Kings 6:16-17*

When angels appear, do they make themselves physically visible to humans, or does God selectively open the eyes of people to see them? Here are other Biblical examples:

> *"Then the LORD opened Balaam's eyes, and he saw the angel of the LORD standing in the road with his sword drawn. So he bowed low and fell facedown." Numbers 22:31*

> *"An angel of the Lord appeared to them, and the glory of the Lord shone around them, and they were terrified." Luke 2:9*

> *"Suddenly an angel of the Lord appeared and a light shone in the cell. He struck Peter on the side and woke him up. 'Quick, get up!' he said, and the chains fell off Peter's wrists." Acts 12:7*

It is not only angels that seem to be able to appear, but potentially Satan as well:

> *"And no wonder, for Satan himself masquerades as an angel of light." 2 Corinthians 11:14*

As image-bearers, our spirits enable us to know there is a world of good and evil that exists around us. For those who have come to personally know Christ and have the Holy Spirit dwelling within, our discernment about such beings can be that much greater. No one should believe there is a demon behind every bush, but those most vulnerable to negative spiritual influences are likely those who believe Satan and his demons do not exist at all. An unseen enemy is a dangerous threat, but an unseen enemy that you don't believe exists may have its way with you.

Questions for Reflection

Was there a concept or statement in this chapter that struck you the most? Explain why.

What observations or signs do you see that humanity can sense the spiritual realm?

How do people you know explain the reality or presence of good and evil?

If there is a right side to be on in this spiritual battle, what side do you think you are on and how would you know?

CHAPTER 6

The Personalities Behind Good and Evil

As an introductory statement to this chapter I have to say to that you are free to disagree with any element of this. I do not know with certainty the degree of truth behind these matters. There is much mystery to this topic, but there also may be more than we are capable of seeing, especially if our hearts and minds are closed to the potential reality of the spirit world.

Decision Time

Previously, we looked at the possible role of demonic and angelic influences on earth. Satan has many titles, such as the father of lies, the prince of darkness, deceiver, tempter, evil one, and the spirit of the Antichrist. Each of the titles accurately describes aspects of his personhood, but the title that currently expresses Satan's primary objective in the war against God is "Antichrist." Jesus claimed he was the Messiah, the Son of God, and Jesus also clearly proclaimed that he was the only path to the Father:

> *Jesus answered, "I am the way and the truth and the life.*
> *No one comes to the Father except through me." John 14:6*

Frankly, this claim by Jesus is where we have to make a decision and believe Jesus is just who he says he is—the only path to the Father—or we have to write him off as a nut who doesn't know what he is talking about. Any religion that claims Jesus as a great prophet but not the Son of God is already not credible, because if Jesus is not the Son of God as he professed, then Jesus is delusional and all his teachings should be regarded as potentially false. However, if he is the Son of God, and if he is the single pathway to eternity with the Father, then it stands to reason that Satan desires to keep as many people as possible from finding this path. Satan is anti-to-Christ because Jesus is the path to eternity with God. Thus Satan, the spirit of the "Antichrist," has one overarching priority: to keep mankind from knowing and following Jesus. Satan knows that God wishes none to perish, and Satan most likely feels a victory with every soul that he diverts away from God and into an eternal separation from the Father:

> *Jesus said, "For God so loved the world that he gave his one and only Son, that whoever believes in him shall not perish but have eternal life. For God did not send his Son into the world to condemn the world, but to save the world through him. Whoever believes in him is not condemned, but whoever does not believe stands condemned already because he has not believed in the name of God's one and only Son. This is the verdict: Light has come into the world, but men loved darkness instead of light because their deeds were evil. Everyone who does evil hates the light, and will not come into the light for fear that his deeds will be exposed. But whoever lives by the truth comes into the light, so that it may be seen plainly that what he has done has been done through God." John 3:16–21*

Diversions

Jesus was very aware of how many things in this world can knock us off the path of finding him:

> *Jesus said, "Enter through the narrow gate. For wide is the gate and broad is the road that leads to destruction, and many enter through it. But small is the gate and narrow the road that leads to life, and only a few find it." Matt. 7:13*

The narrow gate is the point of entry to heaven, and Jesus claimed that he was the gate. Satan, being the deceiver and father of lies, creates all kinds of diversions to keep us off the narrow road and away from the narrow gate. The war for souls is waged by various deceptions through subtle, and not so subtle, forms of misdirected worship.

With these thoughts in mind, we must consider that people and events taking place in the past, present, and future may well be orchestrated by the unseen world that surrounds us. An important consideration is this: demons can possess people, but most of their influence is far subtler, through thoughts passed on to us:

> *"But I am afraid that just as Eve was deceived by the serpent's cunning, your minds may somehow be led astray from your sincere and pure devotion to Christ." 2 Cor. 11:3*

The devil's very nature is one of lies and deceit, and he uses this to undermine God's desire for an eternal relationship with his creation. God and Satan are unique beings with very real personalities and attributes. If we are to determine the potential influence of Satan and his forces, we need to know his patterns of behavior and be aware that his continual bent is on disrupting people from finding their way into God's kingdom. Jesus summarized these spiritual differences:

> *"The thief (Satan) comes only to steal and kill and destroy; I have come that they may have life, and have it to the full." John 10:10*

Opposing Personalities

There is a method of study called "Apophatic Theology" which essentially attempts to explain God by what he is *not*. (For example, God is not hatred, nor is he evil.) If we consider this approach in understanding the differences between God and Satan, it contrasts the nature of Satan and his demons versus a holy and loving God. Because Scripture says Jesus is the full representation of God, the Antichrist's behaviors are going to be manifested in opposing ways to the character of God and his son Jesus. If we are trying to decipher spiritual forces of good and evil, it is helpful to evaluate the two personalities behind each.

When the Holy Spirit enters someone, part of God enters them as well, and God's Spirit starts to manifest itself through a person's thoughts, actions, and behavior. The following are considered to be manifestations of the Holy Spirit when it indwells a believer's life:

> *"But the fruit of the Spirit is love, joy, peace, patience, kindness, goodness, faithfulness, gentleness and self-control."*
> *Gal. 5:22–23*

Because the Holy Spirit is an equal representation of God and Jesus, then these fruits of the Spirit are also characteristics of God. The spirit of the Antichrist manifests attributes opposed to those of God, so we might consider how the indwelling characteristics of the Holy Spirit would compare to the influences of the spirit of the Antichrist:

Love is opposed by Hatred

Joy is supplanted by Depression

Peace is countered by Anger

Patience gives way to Anxiety

Kindness turns to Aggression

Goodness flips to Depravity

Faithfulness to Deceit

Gentleness to Brutality

Self-control falls to sinful Rebellion

Influences of spiritual forces in our lives need to be evaluated, especially in times of confusion or unexplained negative or irrational thoughts and emotions. Consider the presence of darkness when fear, anxiety, doubt, worry, anger, rage, malice, and oppression exist. Satan is a spirit of fear, and he projects that onto us as well. Anxiety and worry oppose the peace that accompanies faith in God. Rage and malice are part of the personality that wants to kill, steal, and destroy. And oppression directly opposes the freedom promised in Christ.

God's presence creates peace, hope, joy, love, and a sense of freedom. Satan imposes fear and an anxious spirit, coupled with a sense of bondage and no choice but to submit and follow. Cults, gangs, and religions that threaten death to anyone who tries to leave are perfect examples of the personality behind evil, Satan. There are opposing forces at play on this earth, and in our lives. If we can recognize the personalities behind the forces of good and evil, then we can recognize who is at work. Too many of us are merely pawns with no idea that we are engaged in a battle, but the cost of the battle could be our very souls and our eternal destiny.

Familiar Spirits

Consider for a moment that the demonic spirits who occupy the earth have strategies that include keeping families trapped within a system of control. Families get stuck in abusive cycles that get passed on for generations. Modern psychology suggests that the "family of origin" is a huge factor in passing on good, bad, criminal, and even cruel, oppressive trends. Psychology, like some prevalent philosophies of modern sciences, are often centered around excluding God in its evaluations, so when we look at this issue with a science-oriented mindset, we end up believing our environments and genetics create who we are. But, perhaps our environments involve more than merely human relationships. Perhaps the unseen is at work too:

> *"Once you were dead because of your disobedience and your many sins. 2 You used to live in sin, just like the rest of the world, obeying the devil—the commander of the powers in the unseen world. He is the spirit at work in the hearts of those who refuse to obey God." Eph. 2:1–2*

The next Scripture suggests that some family blessings and curses are passed on from generation to generation:

> *God says, "I lavish unfailing love to a thousand gen-*
> *erations. I forgive iniquity, rebellion, and sin. But I do not*
> *excuse the guilty. I lay the sins of the parents upon their*
> *children and grandchildren; the entire family is affected—*
> *even children in the third and fourth generations." Ex. 34:7*

Is there a spiritual component to these blessings and curses? Could it be that some "blessings" come with a spiritual wall of protection, including angelic forces that follow and protect individuals and families from demonic havoc? On the other hand, are curses or deeply seated sin tendencies within families carried on from generation to generation by influences of spirits that have become very familiar with a family and its bents? The Bible does not state specifically that this is the case, but perhaps our human experience indicates this may be an influence. As a human, we have a free will, and our free will is potentially capable of stepping out of destructive patterns of behavior, but maybe our wills are not as free as we would like to think. If we have contrary spirits that follow family lines, perhaps it is more than just our will that we are battling.

Many psychologists would say that we reproduce the same situations as our families of origin because we were essentially trained by our environmental situations, and thus we model them. This certainly has elements of truth to it, but when we truly hate certain damaging behaviors within our families of origin, maybe the influence to continue these undesirable and even detestable traits are results of spirits that have gotten a foothold in our family lines. Therefore, we see curses being passed on to the third and fourth generation. Could it be that it is hard to break these curses because they are being put upon us from familiar spirits that follow our families as a way of keeping us captive to sin and away from God?

The bottom line to consider is this: Are the destructive patterns of behavior seen in family lines simply learned behavior because of our environment, or are our environments influenced by spirits that are assigned to tribes and families to keep them away from a path toward God? Conceivably, some of our battles did not start with us. Some of our bents and inclinations are not merely a product of our own personality or learned behavior but spiritually induced. Spiritual strongholds, if they exist, are not typically going to be vanquished by our own wills. When we say someone has great willpower it may not really be that they have great power on their own. It has been my personal experience that it takes my will, in conjunction with God's power, to overcome strongholds. As the Apostle Paul wrote:

> *"I put this in human terms because you are weak in your natural selves. Just as you used to offer the parts of your body in slavery to impurity and to ever-increasing wickedness, so now offer them in slavery to righteousness leading to holiness. When you were slaves to sin, you were free from the control of righteousness. What benefit did you reap at that time from the things you are now ashamed of? Those things result in death! But now that you have been set free from sin and have become slaves to God, the benefit you reap leads to holiness, and the result is eternal life. For the wages of sin is death, but the gift of God is eternal life in Christ Jesus our Lord." Rom. 6:19–23*

When Satan Became Anti-to-Christ

I realize these thoughts and concepts may be very new to some of you. With this in mind, I feel it would be prudent to define a few things and walk through a progression of ideas. First, the spirit of antichrist is Satan, and his work is carried out by other fallen angels that we call demons. The reason they are against, or *anti*-to-Christ, is because of their hatred toward God, and thus they wish to disrupt God's desire to be in relationship with mankind.

This warfare has been going on from the time of Adam and Eve. Satan deceived Adam and Eve, and he has been doing the same to mankind ever since. His tactics for warfare have taken on a very determined path since the birth of Christ. Because Christ offers a pathway to an eternal existence with God, it has forced Satan to create strategies to come against Christ and keep us from him.

Let's ponder a brief history regarding this warfare and consider the birth of Jesus. When the Magi (wise men) came to worship baby Jesus in Bethlehem, they informed Herod (king of the region) about the newborn child who was to become the prophesized messianic leader and king of Israel. This news of a prophesized king was alarming to Herod. A new king and Messiah left Herod in fear for his throne, his leadership, and his power over the people. We can't know with certainty, but perhaps Satan was listening in on this conversation between Herod and the wise men who were searching for the Christ child. If he was, then it would naturally be his desire to kill the child, thus thwarting God's plans for the Messiah to save mankind. Perhaps voices in Herod's head were coming from demons? Perhaps it was because of Satan's influence that Herod decided to kill all boys under the age of two in the town of Bethlehem in an attempt to kill the child?

> *"When Herod realized that he had been outwitted by the Magi, he was furious, and he gave orders to kill all the boys in Bethlehem and its vicinity who were two years old and under, in accordance with the time he had learned from the Magi." Matt. 2:16*

We are told that Jesus's father, Joseph, was warned in a dream to take the child to Egypt for his safety, just prior to Herod's hideous execution of innocent children:

> *"When they had gone, an angel of the Lord appeared to Joseph in a dream. 'Get up,' he said, 'take the child and his mother and escape to Egypt. Stay there until I tell you, for Herod is going to search for the child to kill him.' " Matt. 2:13*

The boys under the age of two in the town where Jesus was born were slaughtered. Was this event because of a warped King's mind, or was he under the influence of the spirit of the Antichrist?

As we move forward in time, just as Jesus was about to begin his ministry, he went into the desert for forty days of fasting in preparation for his ministry. After these forty days, Jesus was likely feeling exceedingly weak and, from the duration of the fast, nearing death. Satan took the opportunity to tempt him by offering him food, worldly power, and prestige. Jesus resisted, and Satan promised that he would return at an opportune time:

> *"When the devil had finished all this tempting, he left him until an opportune time." Luke 4:13*

Perchance, this opportune time was the night before Jesus's crucifixion when Satan entered Judas who betrayed Jesus:

> *"As soon as Judas took the bread, Satan entered into him. 'What you are about to do, do quickly,' Jesus told him."* *John 13:27*

Satan may very well have believed that he ended Jesus's influence when Jesus died on the cross. The opposite was true. Jesus' death and resurrection opened a pathway for all men and women to have an eternal relationship with God. Jesus disarmed the powers of sin, death, and the Devil:

> [Referring to Jesus] *"And having disarmed the powers and authorities, he made a public spectacle of them, triumphing over them by the cross." Colossians 2:15*

From this point forward, Satan's objective is to detour mankind from the true path to God, Jesus. The nature of these detours is nearly endless. Wealth, comfort, power, self-centeredness, false gods, false religions, shame, guilt, and pride are part of an endless array of strategies created to keep us off the path of an eternal existence with our Creator.

Life Story

The following was my response to a social media post from a professor of theology who is a dear friend. This was written within forty-eight hours of the shooting that occurred at Marjory Stoneman Douglas High School in Florida. In one sense this specific event has little significance on a grand scale because these events continue to show themselves in our very lost world. My friend and countless others had to process this tragedy in the best way we knew how. I happened to process it in writing.

> *Oddly, most of America sits back and seem puzzled about why we have the gun violence we do. The onslaught of recent police and school shootings never leave the front pages of the news. We have to be honest with ourselves, guns have been part of America since its foundation, yet never before have we had this level of violence. The guns themselves are nothing more than pieces of hardware that in the right hands, or should we say in the "right minds," create no violence at all. In the possession of the "wrong minds," they become potential instruments of destruction. The question is not what has happened with guns, but what has happened to the minds of Americans?*
>
> *The moral and behavioral demise of the United States has been steady, but the acceleration of events is likely to continue because the foundation of what once anchored this country in moral beliefs is rapidly becoming a minority voice and is too often shunned by the media and many politicians. When gun violence (and violence as a whole) was at its lowest levels in this country, we shared a common morality based on the Bible. Yes, we have had decades of influx from other cultures and other religious belief systems, but the primary source of our trouble is not imported. Our demise is taking place internally through the replacement of a living and active God with the religion of secularism where there is no God except man's wisdom.*
>
> *The progression of secularism includes the following beliefs:*
>
> *Science and evolutionary theory have proven there is no God.*
>
> *If there is no God, there certainly is no Satan.*
>
> *Because there is no God, there is no governing moral authority.*
>
> *We are all biological creatures walking this planet with unique views of truth and no moral absolutes.*

As a whole, humankind should be able to work out its own problems. All we need to do is just try harder.

Interwoven with all of this is the fact that if there is no God and no moral authority, then morality is relative to what each person believes. If we all have our own view of what is right because there is no foundation for truth, then we will continually be at odds with one another. The problem is, if you live with a secular worldview, there is no hope outside of mankind. If you have not noticed, man is not kind, nor will mankind ever be kind on its own volition. Without God's foundation of truth, the future for this nation is one giant crapshoot, and in the end those with power prevail at the expense of the masses. The leadership of North Korea is a great example of no adherence to moral absolutes. Kim Jong Un is a nuclear threat to the world and possesses a similar disregard for life as the mass shooters we have encountered in this country.

On a final note, the most recent school shooting in Florida was by a deceived mind. The shooter claims to have heard demons instruct him how to carry out his deed. Law enforcement involved in the investigation referred to the alleged voices as "demons," and said Cruz, claimed that they told him what he needed to do to launch the deadly assault.

For most of us, we were taught in our education system that science has replaced God. Our secular society has ruled out God and in doing so it has to rule out Satan and his demons as well. When a shooting happens, we always have to consider mental illness, but when those diagnosing the situation have no belief in Satan, the root of some tragedies may be ignored. Mental illness certainly can play a role in some cases of violence, but I also believe manipulation of a person's thoughts can be stirred by demonic input. Frankly, in a secular society these claims about demon's voices are ruled out as quickly as God is ruled out as a solution to the problem.

Do whatever you want with guns, but our troubles are just beginning as Satan increasingly gains a foothold. His personality is on display, and we are losing the indwelling presence of Holy Spirit as we move away from God as a nation. The contrast between good and evil is evident for all who have eyes to see. The separation between light and darkness is becoming more defined, and we need to be careful not to place our trust in a nation, but in God alone.

Jesus said, "The thief comes only to steal and kill and destroy; I have come that they may have life and have it to the full." John 10:10

Doc B

No doubt there is good and evil active in this world. We are at a disadvantage of not being able to tangibly see these forces with our own eye, but you don't necessarily need your physical eyes to see. You need to invite the Holy Spirit to be your eyes so you can discern what God vs. Satan are up to in our world today:

"As it is written: 'God gave them a spirit of stupor, eyes so that they could not see and ears so that they could not hear, to this very day' " Rom. 11:8

Questions to Consider:

Was there a concept or statement in this chapter that struck you the most? Explain why.

What evidence do you see to support the idea that there are personalities behind good and evil?

If there are familiar spirits associated with your family can you decipher what they are?

If you do not believe in Satan and his demons, are you more or less likely to be deceived by him if they do exist? Explain why.

CHAPTER 7

Religion vs Relationship

The Church and Antichurch

SATAN SEEMS TO BE more flagrant in various settings and in certain situations. Dependent on the situation, he has many ways of diverting us from Christ. Some of those diversions exist in cults, secular philosophies, world religions, and even religious doctrines within Christianity. Paul warned the early church about this:

> *"See to it that no one takes you captive through hollow and deceptive philosophy, which depends on human tradition and the basic principles of this world rather than on Christ." Col. 2:8*

I am convinced that Jesus never came to start a religion. Jesus gave his life to open a door to form a relationship with those who seek God and want to have him involved in this earthly life, and the life to come. The Church of Christ Jesus is not a building. The Church is all those (past, present, and future) who believe in Jesus as their Lord and Savior. Unfortunately, various Christian denominational doctrines have elements within them that were created by men as an attempt to control, much like a government would make rules to control its subjects. Some of that control comes from a desire to help members of that denomination lead more godly lives, but other forms of control are oriented around power structures that place power in the hands of men (quite literally) rather than in the hands of God. Satan tends to be very effective at using power for destructive purposes, even within churches. The truth is, we are told to come to Christ directly, as our high priest and intercessor with God:

> "Therefore, since we have a great high priest who has gone through the heavens, Jesus the Son of God, let us hold firmly to the faith we profess. For we do not have a high priest who is unable to sympathize with our weaknesses, but we have one who has been tempted in every way, just as we are—yet was without sin." Heb. 4:14–15

> "Let us then approach the throne of grace with confidence, so that we may receive mercy and find grace to help us in our time of need." Heb. 4:16

No man or woman, regardless of position within any church, has the authority to be God's direct intercessor for us. We are to go directly to Jesus, and others who have gone before us may help us on this path, but our prayers are not to saints nor through some other figures within the church. Nowhere in Scripture does Jesus suggest anything other than a direct relationship with him. It's not that others can't pray for us and give us good advice, but man is not to be placed as spokesmen between us and our direct relationship with the high priest, Jesus.

Equality in the Eyes of God

Scripture supports the truth that we are all equal in the eyes of God. We are all equal because we are part of his creation and we are all fallen because of our sin nature. Regardless of how we try to live our lives, we are all unworthy on our own account to come into the presence of a holy God:

> "This righteousness from God comes through faith in Jesus Christ to all who believe. There is no difference, for all have sinned and fall short of the glory of God, and are justified freely by his grace through the redemption that came by Christ Jesus." Romans 3:22–24

Jesus is the one that restores our relationship with the Triune God. The Holy Spirit is the third person in this holy threesome. When we give our lives to Christ, the Holy Spirit enters us. This gives us an opportunity to have an inner connection with God that can only be experienced when it actually becomes a living reality. It doesn't matter from where you start (a Buddhist, Mormon, Jehovah Witness, atheist, agnostic, etc.) because until we come into relationship with Christ and are filled with the Holy Spirit, we are all lost and separated from God because of the power of sin and death. But thankfully, God has created a path of forgiveness and repentance through Jesus Christ; therefore, Satan has and will continue to try to disrupt this path.

Islam

In observing world history and religions from a vantage point of spiritual warfare, it is my impression that the second largest religion in the world today was potentially a planned diversionary path away from Jesus. Although Islam holds Jesus as being a great prophet, they believe that Jesus did *not* die on the cross, and that Judas died in his place. This alone effectively strips Jesus of being the prophesied Messiah and the son of God. If this is true, then Jesus is not who he says he is and there is no salvation found in him:

> *The Apostle Paul wrote: "And if Christ has not been raised, our preaching is useless and so is your faith." 1 Cor. 15:14*

In various religions, Satan often allows certain attributes of Jesus' character, power, and reign to be seen, but he diverts people off course just enough to keep them from recognizing Jesus as the Savior and the path to God. Keeping us separated from Jesus is Satan's overall plan. This plan takes many different forms, but the true nature of it is always anti-to-Christ. The fact that Islam and Mormonism both give credit to angels giving specific revelation to their prophets, in isolation, away from any other people, leaves me wondering about Paul's warning centuries before:

> *"And no wonder, for Satan himself masquerades as an angel of light. It is not surprising, then, if his servants masquerade as servants of righteousness. Their end will be what their actions deserve." 2 Cor. 11: 14–15*

Anything that causes people to miss Christ must be suspect of spiritual activity, and these religions have elements that divert people away from Christ. Both religions also have histories of killing those who leave the faith, and both have doctrines of "salvation" that divert people away from Jesus and toward their founders. There are many parallels between these religions, although if you go to the official website of the Church of Latter-Day Saints you will find that Mormonism has morphed considerably from its roots with its founder Joseph Smith. Today it more closely, but not entirely, reflects more orthodox Christian doctrines. Mormonism has changed because they believe they can change as they grow in new revelation. I do believe you can be a true follower of Christ and claim to be a Mormon, but the foundation of this religion has suspicious beginnings. Islam, on the other hand, considers it blasphemous to change anything in their holy books, even to the point that some believe it should only be printed and read in Arabic, which the common person is not able to read. In Islam, to alter a holy book's teaching could be met with death.

The God of the Bible and the god of Islam are markedly different. Very simplistically, Allah (the God of Islam) and Jehovah (the Jewish and Christian God) do not have the same personalities. Allah is generally a distant God. According to Allah, our good works in this life may be the only thing that gives you a chance for paradise. In contrast, Jehovah is not distant. In fact, he will indwell you with his very Spirit so you always have access to him in thought and in prayer. Jesus teaches us to love our enemies and lay down our life for others, as Christ did for us. On the other hand, radical Islam, when lived-out to the fullest extent of their holy books, says to kill non-believers. In fact, the Islamic extremists' primary targets for elimination are the Jews and Christians. Hang with me on this point: if you were Satan and you hated God and you wanted to cause as much grief to God as you can, wouldn't you want to kill the Jews who were his chosen people and the lineage of the prophesized Messiah? Wouldn't you also want to be rid of Christians because they are the ones now leading others to the narrow gate of Jesus?

You may think this is a big fairytale. But if there is a god of Islam and a God of the Bible, then what God do you want to serve? Their philosophies of life and death are often diametrically opposed. I have read the Quran, and there is much good in it, but there are also things written that are oppressive, fear-oriented, and murderous. The same may seem to be present in the Old Testament of the Bible if context is not fully understood, but regardless Christ came to show us God's desired path.

Under Christ you have a free will, and there is a celebration when you come to know Jesus and the Holy Spirit enters you. When the Holy Spirit enters you, God then resides within. Is it any wonder that in Islam Allah is described as distant and often impersonal? He does not dwell in anyone, nor does he care to. Through Jesus, God fills you with his own Spirit in order to be in relationship with you, and because of this relationship, he forgives you of your continuous ungodliness. The other god is distant, generally impersonal, and ultimately going to judge you based on your deeds, and his like or dislike for you. If there is one true God, with a distinct personality, is it manifested through Jesus and his Father, or through Allah? If there is only one God, then who is behind the other personality?

Further Perspective

For some additional context, after reading the Quran it would be my estimation that Mohammed was a rather peaceful man at the age of forty, when he had his conversations with the angel in a cave. The early writings of Mohammed that were composed while living in Mecca were much more peaceful in nature, and they often paralleled some of the philosophies found in the Bible. But things changed in his later writings when he moved to Medina. In Medina, he became more of a conquering warrior. This transformation caused him to have shifting beliefs, and these beliefs show up in his writings. His later writings more often suggest killing infidels and other harsh philosophies. A warrior mentality of "submit or die" became more of his motto. Within Islam it is believed that Mohammed's later writings, if in conflict with earlier writings, would take precedence. The later writings overrule the earlier writings because they are viewed as newer revelations. If you only read Mohammed's earlier writings, you would most likely believe that Islam is a religion of peace. But if the later writings supersede the earlier writings, then Radical Islamists have every right to believe their murderous, terroristic actions are just, according to their holy books. Fortunately, God has written certain elements of his peaceful nature into the hearts of mankind so even with instructions toward violence and oppression many are not pulled into these behaviors that grieve the one true God.

The Ultimate Belief in Christian Salvation

As followers of Christ, we are called to lay down our lives for the furtherance of drawing others to Jesus. We believe that Jesus Christ is the only way to heaven, and our heavenly Father wishes that none of his creation would perish. Ultimately, we understand that until someone comes into relationship with Jesus Christ and is filled with the Holy Spirit, he or she will not enter heaven. We also believe that once someone is filled with the Holy Spirit, nothing will separate them from their loving God:

> *"In reply Jesus declared, 'I tell you the truth, no one can see the kingdom of God unless he is born again.'" John 3:3*

> *"Neither height nor depth, nor anything else in all creation, will be able to separate us from the love of God that is in Christ Jesus our Lord." Rom. 8:39*

If being "radical" means following exactly what is written in your holy books, then being a radical for Islam and being a radical for Jesus may have opposing outcomes. In Radical Islam, an unbeliever's life can be taken simply for not converting to Islam, but in Radical Christianity the ultimate expression of Christ's teachings could result in the following response from a Spirit-filled child of God:

> *If I was going to be killed by a non-believing criminal and I was also armed, would I let them take my life? I must consider this because I know I am going to heaven when I die, and this non-believer will go to hell if I kill them first, because they do not have an eternally sealed relationship with Jesus yet. It would be better that I die so that this person may still yet have a chance to find Christ before they die. My father wishes that none should perish, so I will give this person a chance to be saved, because I know when I die I will go into a glorious new life with Christ as I come into God's heavenly kingdom.*

This is radical in the deepest sense because it opposes all our fleshly instincts, but it also mimics Christ's willful substitutionary death on the cross so we could all be saved. This is the result of living a Christ-centered belief system. The ultimate sacrifice as a follower of Christ is to lay down our lives for the salvation of others. In radical Islam the ultimate sign of obedience may be to kill those who do not conform to Islam, even if it means you become a martyr in the process. Contrary to Radical Islam, Jesus and his Father command us not to kill people because they are made in his image and therefore have inherent dignity and great value:

> *"Whoever sheds human blood, by humans shall their blood be shed; for in the image of God has God made mankind."*
> *Genesis 9:6*

Which "God/god " is behind these two belief systems? The self-sacrificial calling for radical Christ followers and the self-glorifying command for radical Islamic followers are in opposition to each other. No doubt the personality behind each philosophy and belief system is not the same person.

Christian Battle

Once someone comes into a relationship with Christ and the Holy Spirit enters in, you might think spiritual battles are over. Well, the battle for the soul may be over as God's Spirit has marked His children for eternity, but the battle for influence to undermine our testimony to those seeking truth may be just beginning. I have a friend who once was into the demonic realm of the occult, and she would allow "spirits" to speak through her to those who paid her for the spirit's advice. As she channeled the thoughts of these spirits on to others, these spirits behaved in a friendly manner to her. However, at one point in her life Jesus (through the Holy Spirit) began to draw her away from this life as a channeler of demonic spirits. These spirits that had been friendly to her began to become aggressive and threatening toward her as she was being drawn toward Jesus. She ended up giving her life to Christ, but she expressed that there were times that these spirits were seeking her out again. Fortunately, most of us will not be in a situation where demonic influences are so evident and dramatic, but whether dramatic or not, we live in a world full of clever diversions created to keep us from Christ.

I have two brothers in Christ who are pastors for the gospel of Jesus Christ in Pakistan. As we discussed demons, they shared that family members of Christians and non-Christians alike often request their ministry team to cast out demons that have come to rest in a loved one. They said the demons are often very threatening with loud, aggressive voices to attempt to scare those who are going to intercede in Jesus' name. The pastors ignore the threats and lay hands on the person in the name of Jesus, and just as is noted in the New Testament, some demons shriek as they depart.

Demons exist and demonic "possession" is sometimes outwardly visible, but demonic "influence" is more subtle and may come to bear on us all, especially through our thought-life. Demons have been present since their fall from heaven, and their influence on mankind was as evident in Jesus's day as it is in our day:

"When he saw Jesus from a distance, he ran and fell on his knees in front of him. He shouted at the top of his voice, "What do you want with me, Jesus, Son of the Most High God? Swear to God that you won't torture me!" For Jesus had said to him, 'Come out of this man, you evil spirit!' Then Jesus asked him, 'What is your name?' 'My name is Legion,' he replied, 'for we are many. And he begged Jesus again and again not to send them out of the area." Mark 5:6–10

Because those of us filled with the Holy Spirit are most likely to be the hands and mouthpiece of Jesus in this world, Satan also wants to limit our effectiveness. There may be no greater witness to the presence of the Holy Spirit than a transformed life. The Bible gives us many examples of this with Paul being the most notable. He went from being a murderer of Christ's followers to the one who spread the good news of Christ to *all* people, regardless of their ethnicity, socio-economic status, etc.

Keep in mind also the Apostle Peter. He abandoned Christ just hours before the crucifixion, but once filled with the Holy Spirit, he boldly proclaimed Christ. Like the other disciples, he met his death proclaiming Jesus' lordship rather than denying him again. Since the personal witness of anyone filled with the Spirit is powerful, Satan wants to take that testimony away. Teachers and witnesses for Christ become targets for Satan. Satan knows that he will not retrieve this soul for himself, but he would like to shut them up. There is a spiritual battle, and Satan would like all Christ's followers to fall before our fellow man and lose our ability to witness because of our moral failures:

"For our struggle is not against flesh and blood, but against the rulers, against the authorities, against the powers of this dark world and against the spiritual forces of evil in the heavenly realms." Eph. 6:12

Consider for a moment that all people use their personalities to influence others in one way or another, whether we realize it or not. You and I will each use what is built up within us to influence others. Conceivably, Satan uses fear and anxiety as primary weapons to oppress people physically, mentally, and spiritually because this is what he himself experiences. Consider that Satan may exist in a perpetual state of fear and anxiety because he does not know the time or place of his final judgement. He does know that his end is coming, but God is the only one who knows the time. As Satan exists in his perpetual state of unknowing, his game plan is to damage the Creator in the most effective way he knows, to disrupt and destroy the link between the Father and his creation. The following verse certainly can be taken as a warning of Satan's influence all around us:

> *"Religion that God our Father accepts as pure and faultless is this: to look after orphans and widows in their distress and to keep oneself from being polluted by the world."*
> *James 1:27*

Because Satan is the prince of this world, and the father of lies, not being polluted by the world means to stay away from everything that has the spirit of the Antichrist associated with it. To understand what these things are, we need to know the character of God and the character of Satan. Once we know the characteristics of both, we need to learn to apply this knowledge by identifying the potential spiritual forces behind events in our days and in our world.

Life Story

Many things can interfere with experiencing a life-giving relationship with God who wants intimacy with us. Through Jesus, we can become adopted members of God's family, sons and daughters of God. We become children of the King. However, lies from the devil try to keep us from entering this true and trustworthy eternal relationship. In a sense, we exit in fog, only able to dimly see the spiritual reality of this life. I feel the following life event is a good metaphor of what too often hinders our view of reality.

I don't remember my exact age, but I was in elementary school, most likely around the age of eight or nine. My best friend, Rick, and I loved adventures, and we often escaped on our bicycles for hours on end. One evening as it was nearing dusk, we rode to our elementary school. There was a soccer field, baseball diamond, and an expanse of a public park adjacent to the school. All this area was open to us for adventurous rides on our bikes. As we rounded the corner of the school and were about to leave the cement sidewalk and pedal out into the expanse of open playground, we saw the area was covered in a dense layer of fog. Looking back on this experience, I have seen a lot of fog in my lifetime, but nothing quite like this. Even though the fog was only from ground level to about four or five feet high, it was so dense that we could hardly see beyond five yards in front of us. We quickly learned that if we stood upright on our pedals, our head would pop out above the fog, but if we were to bend our knees and lower ourselves onto our seats, our head and body would completely disappear into the thick fog.

With great excitement we looked at one another, and without a spoken word we charged full steam ahead on our bikes into the fog-laden field. It was rather comical as we raced off in different directions, buzzing around the field on our bikes, completely concealed by the fog except when we stood on our pedals. We would call out to one another in order to know where the other was amidst the fog, but unless we stood on our pedals at the same time, we could not see each other. I remember standing on our pedals at the same moment, seeing one another's heads gliding along the top of the fog, only to disappear when we dropped down onto the seats of our bikes again. We literally wore ourselves out racing about the fields, looking up often to be sure we were not going to run into a goal post, a tree, or some other unwanted object.

As I reflect on this memory, I certainly remember the joy of that foggy adventure, especially since it is not something I have ever been able to duplicate. It was truly one of those times when you had to be there to fully appreciate it. Yet as I have thought more deeply about this event, I realize it had some powerful parallels to our walk with God. Honestly, most of the time we are living in a fog, sitting on the seats of our bikes as we ride through life. Life can seem unclear, difficult, or "foggy," and while in the fog of the world we lose our vision. To see over the fog of our lives requires the presence of the Holy Spirit within us. This is the only thing that can grant us God's perspective of reality, rather than our own foggy perspective of life. The Holy Spirit is our pedals to stand on, allowing the truth of God to penetrate our hearts and give us the power to stand above our circumstances. Unfortunately, we don't often enough take a moment to rely on our Spirit-pedals to see over the fog of this world and obtain a fuller view of God's reality. While in the fog, we are blinded to many things, and we may even run into obstacles that could have been avoided if we had stood on our Spirit-pedals to gain God's perspective.

In my opinion, many of us have likely received Jesus and welcomed the Spirit to indwell us, but we may not allow the Spirit to truly guide our direction, to be our pedals. The gift of the Spirit within us is given to us which allows us to be in an ongoing relationship with God. And it is only when we are engaging in this relationship with God that we are given glimpses above the fog. What a beautiful and exhilarating feeling it is to stand on our pedals and see above the fog as God clears away the clouds in our hearts, minds, and spirits.

Questions to Consider

Was there a concept or statement in this chapter that struck you the most? Explain why.

If you are a follower of Christ, why would Satan want to disrupt your life?

If sin taints us all, and Christ is the only means of being redeemed from our sins, then explain why God's enemy (the Antichrist) wants to distract us away from a faith in Christ?

How does Satan distract you?

CHAPTER 8

The Spirit Within

MORE THAN A DECADE ago I was part of creating a ministry called Lookup2him. The premise of the ministry is super simple, almost childlike. LookUp2him sends short text messages containing Scripture verses seven times a day for forty days, and the purpose of the messages is to remind you to reconnect with God. If you involved yourself in deliberate communication seven times a day for the next forty days do you think you would experience more of the personal nature of our God? Those who have done this find it to be true.

LookUp2him's core premise is that God is faithful to respond to you if you engage in a sincere desire to know him. The ministry's foundation is represented by Jesus' words in John 14:6 and Matthew 7:7–8. Simply put, in John 14:6 Jesus says the way to a relationship with the Father is through him. This is necessary because it is through this relationship that the Holy Spirit is poured out into a person's life. In Matthew 7:7–8 Jesus is very directly saying that if we ask, seek, and knock, He and his Father will respond. It is simple, but honestly, we need simple . . . and God knows that.

> *"Jesus answered, 'I am the way and the truth and the life. No one comes to the Father except through me.'" John 14:6*

> *"Ask and it will be given to you; seek and you will find; knock and the door will be opened to you. For everyone who asks receives; he who seeks finds; and to him who knocks, the door will be opened." Matt. 7:7–8*

Jesus makes it clear that if you truly are seeking a relationship with him and you knock at his door and ask for a relationship, he will show up. As we reviewed in earlier chapters, many adults won't or don't take this promise seriously because of all the walls and barriers we have built up that hinder our faith. We feel safe with the box of beliefs we created. Because of this, we stick with the status quo regarding our relationship with Jesus and the Father. It is a sad state of affairs to be offered a relationship with our Creator and then turn it down, or at best restrict it because of the small boxes of faith we have built for ourselves. A major challenge for many is that a childlike faith requires having a childlike trust:

> *"And without faith it is impossible to please God because anyone who comes to him must believe that he exists and that he rewards those who earnestly seek him." Heb. 11:6*

> *"Jesus said, '"Yet a time is coming and has now come when the true worshipers will worship the Father in spirit and truth, for they are the kind of worshipers the Father seeks."' John 4:23*

Jesus gave his life so that you and I have a pathway to an intimate and eternal relationship with the Father. If your heart is truly seeking to know God, through Jesus, he will answer you in ways that will make his presence real. If you are knocking at God's door because your heart's desire is to be taken in as a child of the King, then he will open the door so that relationship can begin. The heart is the key to a relationship with God. If your heart is drawn to God, Jesus is saying to ask, seek, and knock, and through the Holy Spirit God will make himself known. When you invite Jesus in, an undeniable presence will enter and start to transform your life into a life that begins to grow by the power of the Spirit. God and Jesus are awaiting our childlike faith so that we can become eternal children of the King:

> *"Yet to all who received him, to those who believed in his name, he gave the right to become children of God—children born not of natural descent, nor of human decision or a husband's will, but born of God." John 1:12–13*

Fruit of the Spirit

Paul wrote about some of the manifestations of the presence of the Holy Spirit within a person's life in Galatians 5:22–24:

> *"But the fruit of the Spirit is love, joy, peace, patience, kindness, goodness, faithfulness, gentleness and self-control."*

Paul went on to say in the next sentence:

> *"Against such things there is no law. Those who belong to Christ Jesus have crucified the sinful nature with its passions and desires."*

Granted, when you enter this relationship you will not manifest all fruits of the Spirit, nor will your sinful nature disappear with the wave of a magic wand. Typically, God does not send his Spirit into you and make you instantaneously all well. Rather, God sends his Spirit into you to begin a relational journey of growth and transformation. You become a child of his, and like a good father, he is there to guide you into what is good.

Few people who enter this relationship will have an immediate, overwhelming, transformative experience. However, some people literally are saved, changed, and freed from bondages and strongholds instantaneously. Experientially, most of us experience a more gradual transformation, and often this transformation comes with levels of growing pains. Pain, whether it be physical or emotional, redirects our lives and activities. The beauty of transformational pain is that when you get to look back in time, you see how these events created good. Consequently, you are actually grateful for the pain that caused the transformation. Most certainly you don't want to repeat the pain, but the resulting changes in the course of your life make the pains worth it. As Paul explained to the early believers:

> *"Now the Lord is the Spirit, and where the Spirit of the Lord is, there is freedom. And we, who with unveiled faces all reflect the Lord's glory, are being transformed into his likeness with ever-increasing glory, which comes from the Lord, who is the Spirit." 2 Cor. 3:17–18*

As mentioned in previous chapters, we all have to consider the spiritual battle for the hearts, minds, and souls of humanity. Consider Scripture's emphasis that the only way to be sure you are on the side of God, in which eternal salvation is offered, is if you come to a saving faith in Jesus.

The Trinity Within Us

If you have made Jesus Lord and have entered into a personal relationship with him, then the Holy Spirit has entered, and you have within you the potential to interact with the Holy Trinity on an internal level:

> *"Then Jesus came to them and said, 'All authority in heaven and on earth has been given to me. Therefore go and make disciples of all nations, baptizing them in the name of the Father and of the Son and of the Holy Spirit, and teaching them to obey everything I have commanded you. And surely I am with you always, to the very end of the age.'" Matt. 28:18–20*

The interaction and relationship between the Father, Son, and Holy Spirit is a mystery in many ways, because our understanding of God is rudimentary at best. God is so far beyond our imagination that even the most studied and mature view of God is infantile as compared to the vast scope of the one who hung the universe in place and created the precision manifested in all life forms we behold on planet Earth.

Although no one except for the members of the Trinity (Father, Son, and Holy Spirit) knows the fullness of their relationship, it is worth the discussion to entertain a potential elementary understanding of the Trinity. For a moment let's view the Trinity like an equilateral triangle. All sides of the triangle are equal and at each point of the triangle resides a member of the Trinity. Thus, residing at the angles are God the Father, Jesus the Christ, and the Holy Spirit. The three are each separate yet they are interwoven in total unity and mutuality. They are of one mind but three separate persons.

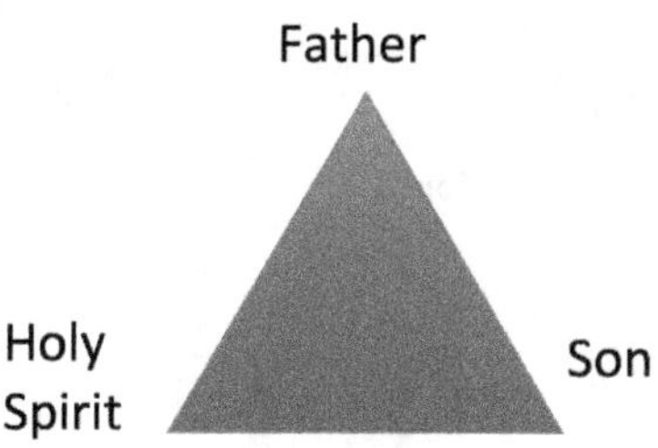

The three individuals are in full communication at all times, and the thoughts of one may be shared simultaneous with the others. Because they are of one mind/will with one unified heart, they all hold the same view of reality. In essence, you would get the same answer to any of your questions from each of them. They all hold a unified view because their very essence is the same. The thoughts of one always reflect the thoughts of the others. To put it into an earthly analogy, they are like three computers hardwired together—each is separate, yet their information can be instantaneously shared between the others and their basis for information is fully unified.

When we invite Jesus Christ into our lives, Jesus promises that we will receive the Holy Spirit. The Holy Spirit becomes our internal connection to the communication within the Trinity. It is as if the triangle was an arrowhead and the Holy Spirit tip plunges into our heart and resides there. Now that the Holy Spirit resides within us, we have a connection to the other two because the three members of the Trinity are in continual, interlacing communication.

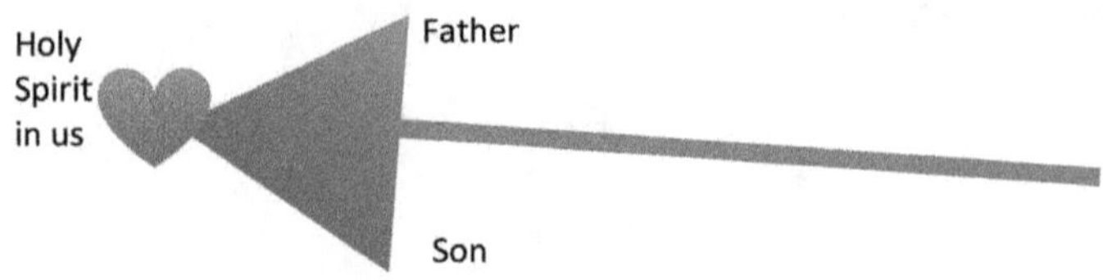

When Jesus walked the earth, the Holy Spirit had not yet been given out to those who believe, so Jesus was the embodiment of the Truth of the Trinity. Once Jesus left, he sent the Holy Spirit to inhabit those who believe. From this point forward, the Holy Spirit became the source of Truth that dwells within us. When the Spirit inhabits us, we have the "potential" to be guided, motivated, and directed by the Father and the Son, by way of the Holy Spirit. As Jesus prepared to leave this earthly realm in physical form, he said this to his disciples:

> *"All this I have spoken while still with you. But the Counselor, the Holy Spirit, whom the Father will send in my name, will teach you all things and will remind you of everything I have said to you." John 14:25–27*

From a graphics standpoint the triangular representation of the Trinity is a very structured symbol, and it expresses only a rudimentary visual concept. However, the relational flow between God, Jesus, and the Holy Spirit is anything but static or rudimentary. The flow and exchange between the Father, Son, and Holy Spirit might better be represented as a flowing, or a continuous form of communication.

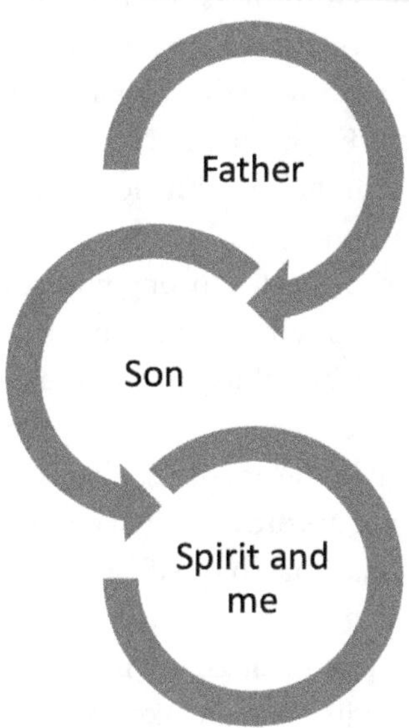

The thing to keep in mind, is that we have an ability to be part of that flow of input and communication from the Trinity once the Spirit enters us. The ageless struggle for those aware of the indwelling of the Spirit is how to live in such a way that this connection becomes alive, real, and undeniable. A life fully immersed in God is contingent upon the entrance of the Holy Spirit, and the entrance of the Holy Spirit is based upon giving our lives to Christ. Once the Holy Spirit enters, we have the "capacity" for an entirely new life filled with the abundant presence of God:

> *"Do you not know that your body is a temple of the Holy Spirit, who is in you, whom you have received from God? You are not your own . . . "* 1 Cor. 6:19

Sin Separates

Despite the presence of the Holy Spirit within us, a multitude of things can interfere with this relationship. Perhaps we can consider "sin" as anything that draws us away from this relationship. Sin pulls us away, but the forgiveness we are granted through Christ breaks down the barriers that sin creates. Because we cannot avoid sin, God has created a pathway through a cycle of repentance and forgiveness to nullify sin. Sin temporarily shuts down, or at best interferes with our communion with God, but repentance and forgiveness opens our union again.

We are our own obstacles to ongoing communication with God because of our self-oriented sin nature. Prior to coming into a relationship with Christ, and thus prior to the entrance of the Holy Spirit, we have an "old self" which may carry with it all kinds of sin propensities. I grew up in the era of sex, drugs, and rock n' roll, and the culture surrounding me drew me in. I am now a new creation in Christ Jesus, but trust me, that "old self" and its propensities are still housed within me. My old self wants to raise its ugly head, and the only way to suppress it is through a willful relinquishment to the Spirit that now dwells within me. It takes very little for most of us to venture back into the old self. When we do, we are shutting down, denying, or hindering our connection with the Spirit because of our sin nature. When this happens the redemptive pathway back is only obtained through repentance and forgiveness, which God has promised us through our relationship with Jesus. Jesus bought our ticket out of a life governed by sin and death. It is only through Jesus that we have forgiveness of our sins, and along with it, the gift of eternal life. The apostle Paul wrote:

> *"You were taught, with regard to your former way of life, to put off your old self, which is being corrupted by its deceitful desires; to be made new in the attitude of your minds; and to put on the new self, created to be like God in true righteousness and holiness." Eph. 4:22–24*

When Paul refers to the "old self," he refers to the human part of us that pridefully, fearfully, or ignorantly remains separated from God. We are corrupted by our fallen nature and are easily lured into our sin nature. Thus, we are prone to shut down the activity of the Spirit within us. The "new self" is only possible when the Spirit enters, and through the Spirit we gain entrance to God's righteousness and holiness (Rom. 6-8). No, we don't become perfect, but we gain entrance into an eternal relationship with the Trinity. Sin then becomes anything that creates separation in this relationship. True freedom comes from releasing all of who we are into the hands of Jesus and then asking him to mold us the way he would like us to be. He is the potter and we are the clay. He crafts us into a vessel that contains, and lives by, his Spirit's influence. When our vessel is filled to overflowing, we then pour his love out onto those around us:

> *"May the God of hope fill you with all joy and peace as you trust in him, so that you may overflow with hope by the power of the Holy Spirit." Rom.* 15:13

The Spirit resides in those who follow Jesus, and our hearts are laid bare before the Trinity. There are no secrets. God's primary concern about any of us is our hearts and minds. God cares less about the external or temporary things in our lives because his focus is on the contents of our heart and soul. Once we are in relationship with the Trinity, it is our hearts and minds that he begins to change. This process of changing the heart of a man or woman is a lifelong process through which God orchestrates events and situations to take us on the path he has set before us. He wants to make us holy, as He is holy, and when we invite him in he takes us on a path that leads us toward holiness. It is our hearts and minds that God is after. When we delight in him, he delights in us. As it is written:

> *"Delight yourself in the LORD and he will give you the desires of your heart." Psalm* 37:4

Transference of Fire

A typical understanding of a life lived for Christ often comes down to a daily prayer and a human attempt to be "good" in God's eye. Too often we are doing things we think God would approve of rather than doing the work he has laid out for us, and we may inaccurately speak for God rather than allowing God to speak through us. It would be nice if God were in the flesh and would tell us day by day, face to face, just what he wanted, but that's not the way things are. A life fully directed by God was only accomplished by one man, Jesus. The title "Transference of Fire" is an analogy to a life lived for Christ. Here is the analogy:

If you take a branding iron and put it in the coals of a very hot fire you will find that with enough time the iron glows as hot as the coals themselves. The fire does not consume the branding iron, as it still maintains its shape and identity. While in the fire, the branding iron does take in the heat energy of the fire, so it becomes as hot as, and visually as red as, the coals that surround it. There is a similar type of synergy between God and those who are immersed in his presence. If we bathe ourselves in his presence, his power and energy can come into us so that we begin to represent his very nature. Just like the fire with the branding iron, he does not take our identity away, but he infuses us with his power so that we can be used for his purposes.

We can only become like Jesus when we place ourselves continually in his presence. Because we are easily drawn away, we too often jump into and out of his presence. Because of this he never really gets to fully take up a continuous energy within us. Sticking with the analogy of the branding iron, it would be as if we moved the iron into and out of the fire and thus the full transference of heat from the fire never takes place. To have God live through us is all about submission and continually placing everything we are into his care.

Jesus overcame the weaknesses of being human by being filled with his Father, by way of the Holy Spirit. He experienced temptation just as we do, but because God cannot be tempted, nor does he tempt anyone, Jesus did not fall into temptation because this is not the nature of God:

> *"When tempted, no one should say, 'God is tempting me.'*
> *For God cannot be tempted by evil, nor does he tempt any-*
> *one." James 1:13*

It is interesting that at Pentecost when the Holy Spirit was first released upon the new Christians, it was described as tongues of flames that rested on people—a transference of fire of sorts:

> *"When the day of Pentecost came, they were all together in one place. Suddenly a sound like the blowing of a violent wind came from heaven and filled the whole house where they were sitting. They saw what seemed to be tongues of fire that separated and came to rest on each of them. All of them were filled with the Holy Spirit and began to speak in other tongues as the Spirit enabled them." Acts 2:1–4*

Walking with God

God's Spirit comes to reside in believing men, women and children. Many of you reading this have had times when you felt God alive on the inside of you and whatever you were doing or thinking at the time was filled with a clarity that only comes from him. So why, as Holy Spirit-filled believers, don't we feel this all the time? Part of this difficulty is that we walk this earth in a fallen realm that is under the continual influence of Satan. Another reason is that many don't know how to walk in his presence, and we certainly don't practice his presence enough. If we are going to be like the branding iron, we must stay in the fire where we are immersed in the mind of the Trinity. To do this we must invite him into our lives continually. Even Jesus, while being fully divine, removed himself and went into the wilderness to spend time with his Father.

> *But Jesus often withdrew to lonely places and prayed.*
> Luke 5:16

If Jesus needed alone time with the Father, how much more so do we? How much time do you spend in communication with God each day?

At the time I am writing this, I have been receiving text message reminders from www.lookup2him.com every two hours for more than 10 years to remind me to look up to him. I don't think this book would be possible for me to write had this not been part of my life. Over this time, I have tried to determine just how a person can maintain an ongoing relationship with Christ without continual reminders to break through the noise of the world. I have concluded that the only way of doing this is to attempt to live in a state of continual gratitude. I have reached this conclusion because ongoing gratitude to God is a type of ongoing prayer. Therefore, ongoing prayer is a form of ongoing communication that allows for regular interaction and communication with the Father and the Son by means of the Holy Spirit.

If you think God has responded to your infrequent prayers, how much more do you think you would experience his presence with ongoing prayer? Please don't make any assumptions that I have somehow overcome the obstacles that interfere with my relationship to the Trinity. I am merely stating that I believe ongoing gratitude is a means for an ongoing relationship within the Trinity. When you are grateful for all things, you are saying that you are trusting God for his hand in all things. I believe this relinquishment of our control over circumstances gives God permission to orchestrate things in our lives for good, even in the difficult times. As I cited earlier:

> *"And we know that in all things God works for the good of those who love him, who have been called according to his purpose." Rom. 8:28*

One thing we must all keep in mind is that God is always there—we are the ones who disconnect from him. We are easily distracted and we pull away, sometimes for minutes and sometimes for days, weeks, and even years. There is a relationship void built in our hearts that can only be filled by God, and this void is part of his design for us, because it draws us towards him with a longing to fill this emptiness. It is sin that separates us from him. It is sin that causes our hearts to cry out for his love and comfort to fill the emptiness created by the separation sin causes. If you think about it, it is a universal tendency for humanity to create its own gods to fill this longing. Yet, none of these gods fill that void except the one true God. By way of his Son, Jesus, the one true

God provides a way for us to connect with him through the Holy Spirit that fills our empty hearts.

Our challenge as we walk this earth is to enter into relationship with God in our thoughts and prayers on an ongoing basis so he can truly live through us. We have to abandon ourselves through continual relinquishment of self if we are to maximize the good he can do *in* us and *through* us. Jesus was the ultimate example of this.

In John 14:24, Jesus taught saying, *"These words you hear are not my own; they belong to the Father who sent me."* In verses 25 and 26 he continues: *"All this I have spoken while still with you. But the Counselor, the Holy Spirit, who the Father will send in my name will teach you all things and will remind you of everything I have said to you."*

Jesus' healing of the sick, raising the dead, giving sight to the blind, hearing to the deaf, etc. were not done outside of God. Everything Jesus did was out of the fact that he, Father, and the Spirit are one person with one mind/will. Jesus also let us know that if we place ourselves in a right relationship within the Trinity, we can do, and are called to do, similar things in this life as he did:

> *"Jesus replied, 'I tell you the truth, if you have faith and do not doubt, not only can you do what was done to the fig tree, but also you can say to this mountain, "Go, throw yourself into the sea," and it will be done.'" Matt. 21:21*

Those who are honest about their sin and failings as a child of God will admit how unworthy they often feel of being in relationship with an infinite and Holy God. Here are the words of Saint Paul the Apostle of Jesus Christ:

> *"I do not understand what I do. For what I want to do I do not do, but what I hate I do. And if I do what I do not want to do, I agree that the law is good. As it is, it is no longer I myself who do it, but it is sin living in me. I know that nothing good lives in me, that is, in my sinful nature. For I have the desire to do what is good, but I cannot carry it out. For what I do is not the good I want to do; no, the evil I do not want to do—this I keep on doing. Now if I do what*

I do not want to do, it is no longer I who do it, but it is sin living in me that does it." Rom. 7:15–20

On a day-to-day basis we have both failures and triumphs in allowing God to dominate our thoughts. This battle begins in the mind, and the mind has many influences upon it, some of which we seem to be able to control and some we must struggle with or against. Fortunately, this journey is not about individual moments. Our journey of growth and refinement is a day-by-day, week-by-week, month-by-month, and year-by-year process. When people pass from this life we frequently review their character and their impact in this world. If they walked with God, they undoubtedly had an impact that went far beyond their personal, daily failures and triumphs. As believers, our lives as a whole hold hope and promise of being used by God in significant ways. We cannot, and should not, sell ourselves short as we struggle to overcome our propensity towards sin. This walk with God is a process of continual refinement, but our progress in this journey is directly related to the closeness we hold with him.

Life Story

God provides us with signs of his presence so that we can be aware he is involved in our day-to-day lives. Like a good father, he likes to lovingly oversee our lives and give us personalized reminders of our relationship with him. It may surprise some of you to hear that, in my experience, God is playful. One way that God has been playfully active in my own life is through a game of lost and found. When things get lost I expect them to be found because God seems to uncover lost things in my life. I have many potential stories about finding things when there seemed to be little hope of discovering them, but let me share an early life experience that I felt God played a role in.

God provided evidence of his presence in my life through an experience I had on a family vacation. If I recall correctly, I was probably ten years of age when my family went on a road trip vacation from Michigan to Colorado. For quite some time, I had wanted a jackknife of my own, but my father generally did not provide these kinds of things for me; he required me to earn the money myself. Options were few for earning money at such a young age, and thus getting a knife was not very likely. Although I did not have a firm, personal relationship with God at this point in my life, I did believe in him. Prior to going on a hike during our vacation, I again expressed to my father the desire I had for a jackknife. Then we set off hiking on a path along a mountain stream. As we were trekking along, I found a really awesome knife. It took some work to get the rust off it, but there was little doubt in my mind that God was the reason for my find. It wasn't just a knife; it was a kid's dream knife for outdoor adventures. It was a multi-tool that included fold out knives, scissors, a leather punch, a screwdriver, a can opener, a spoon, a fork, and a few other special attachments.

When I found the knife, my dad responded that God must have heard my request. This opened both the windows of my heart and my physical eyes to look for God's provision in my life. I truly believe God was the one who laid the knife in my hiking path in advance so that I could enjoy it for years to come. Fifty years later, I still have this same knife because it is a reminder of God's gracious and playful provision, and because it's pretty cool.

In one of my earlier stories, I mentioned how God has tended to do things in a series of threes in my life, just so I can't miss his activity behind it. Finding knives was no different; I found two other knives on this family vacation for a total of three knives! But I confess that none of them were quite as cool as the first one. God is a good, active, and playful father. How have you experienced God in this way?

The story continues: I thought this story about finding the lost was completed as I was writing this at the base of Mary Jane Ski Resort, while waiting for it to warm up. We've had great snow the past few days, so I came here early enough to get good parking on a Friday morning. Since it was minus fifteen degrees when I arrived, I intended to sit in my truck and write this story while waiting for the temperature to become more enjoyable. After I'd spent about ninety minutes writing, it had warmed up to above zero. The Colorado sun was shining brightly, and I was ready to ski. I usually have to take a chairlift to the backside of the mountain and then another chairlift until I can reach the highest point of the resort. As I was skiing my first run of the day to get to the other lift that would bring me to the top of the mountain, something caught my eye in the middle of the run. I stopped, walked a few yards back up the slope, and saw that it was a compact video camera with a special handheld mount for filming purposes. No skiers were above or below me. I was hoping I would see somebody looking for it, but it must have unknowingly fallen out of someone's backpack. I picked it up because I was hoping my gift for finding things might benefit the owner. I did not want to ski with it, so I skied back to my truck, dropped it on the front seat, and went back to my day of skiing. I did call lost and found at the resort to report my finding, along with a phone number where I could be reached. No one claimed it through lost and found but if you read this book and it was yours be sure to let me know, I am saving it for you.

When I say that God is playful, this is exactly what I mean. I was in the midst of writing a story about the way God allows me to find things, and then minutes after writing the story he proves the point by putting a very cool video camera in my skiing path. God is alive and present at all times, but do we see God's activity and acknowledge it to be him? If you have not experienced God's playful side, perhaps you need to invite God into this role. Trust me, he will actively pursue you in relationship as you pursue him in return.

Questions to Ponder

Was there on concept or statement in this chapter that struck you the most? Explain why.

Have you invited Jesus to be Lord of your life? Why or why not?

How effective is your communication within the Trinity?

What interferes with your relationship to the Trinity most?

What changes in your life would you like to see to make this relationship more continuous?

CHAPTER 9

The Battle for Our Mind

The Battle Within

WE HAVE EXPLORED THE concept of the "faith of a child," which Jesus said was necessary to see the kingdom of God at work. We also explored the walls our adult minds have created and how they prevent us from having the faith of a child—not just any child, but a child of the King. In addition, we have looked at the possibilities of a spiritually influenced life from a spirit world that is potentially integrated into many aspects of our earthly life. In the previous chapter we emphasized the power, and need, for the entrance of the Holy Spirit into our lives in order to have increased communication with the Father and the Son. We also stressed the fact that it is through the Holy Spirit that we are given availability to the "mind" of the Trinity. Throughout the book we reflected on a definition of "Truth," as being that which aligns with God's perspective of reality. Considering what truth is, we must conclude that in order for our thoughts to be "true" they have to coincide with God's perspective of reality. Therefore, it is only through a living, indwelling, and ongoing relationship with God that we can hope to see more clearly how God views reality/truth.

The indwelling of the Holy Spirit in conjunction with reading and being familiar with the written Word of God is necessary to recognize truth. The Holy Spirit can bring truth into our minds, but we have to be willing to hear it, receive it, and live it, in order for it to be manifested in our lives. The presence of the Holy Spirit gives us a chance of seeing the difference between God's desires and the lies of the world and the deception of our own flesh. It is through the Holy Spirit that we have a chance to respond to life in ways pleasing to the Father rather than following the deception and allure of the Enemy wanting to hold us captive to sin. It has been mentioned before and will be emphasized again to consider "sin" as any thought, action, or behavior that causes a separation between God and us. Regardless of the presence of the Holy Spirit, we all have similar battles, and the battles begin in our minds:

> *"We demolish arguments and every pretension that sets itself up against the knowledge of God, and we take captive every thought to make it obedient to Christ." 2 Cor. 10:5*

Truly understanding the spiritual world that surrounds us is unlikely to be something we will ever grasp because it is not visible to us, but Scripture makes it clear it exists and is active. In consideration of this unseen world and its interaction with us, there seems to be an internal battle *within the mind*, but there is also a battle *for control of the mind*. If left unchecked, spiritual forces may try to control our thoughts in order to make our minds subject to their will. Since Jesus was fully human and experienced an existence like ours, the battle *of* the mind and *for* the mind were also likely part of Jesus's life. If sin is anything that causes us to be separated from God, then Jesus is the model of what humanity can be because he was also fully human yet he did not sin. His divine nature was able to continuously overcome the battles of the flesh and the temptations from Satan. He could not be separated from God the Father:

> *"Jesus said, 'I and the Father are one.'" John 10:30*

> *"For we do not have a high priest who is unable to empathize with our weaknesses, but we have one who has been tempted in every way, just as we are—yet he did not sin." Heb. 4:15*

During the hours before Jesus's crucifixion, Jesus struggled in his own mind and spirit as he imagined enduring his sacrificial death and the separation from the Father he would experience in the three days following. Jesus knew what awaited him on the cross, and he had a chance to bail out, but he elected to follow the will of the Father despite the contrary calls from his flesh and, most likely, tempting voices from Satan. In prayer, he asked:

> *"'Father, if you are willing, take this cup from me; yet not my will, but yours be done.'" Luke 22:42*

As we venture further into the topics of the battle of the mind, our sin nature, and the gifts of repentance and forgiveness, we consider Jesus' final words on the cross:

> *"Father, forgive them, for they do not know what they are doing." Luke 23:34*

As he hung on the cross, Jesus may have been asking God to forgive them for this single act against him, but I believe Jesus' words went much further. I believe Jesus was saying something like this: *Father, I have grown up as a human, seen the stubborn and foolish hearts of men, and taught my disciples for three years, yet have repeatedly witnessed their inability to grasp the reality of who we are. Father, this creation of ours is not all that we thought it should and could be, and we need to forgive them, as they are incapable of not sinning and falling short of what they were designed to be.*

The Apostle Paul wrote:

> *"This righteousness from God comes through faith in Jesus Christ to all who believe. There is no difference, for all have sinned and fall short of the glory of God, and are justified freely by his grace through the redemption that came by Christ Jesus." Rom. 3:22–24*

Jesus's request to the Father to forgive us is what now gives us grace and forgiveness, despite our sin nature. Grace and forgiveness are continually offered to those who embrace Christ, who are filled with the Holy Spirit, and who openly admit and repent of their shortcomings. Jesus was aware of the battle that takes place in the human mind because he experienced it, yet he overcame the battle and was without sin. He is the only human who has ever accomplished this, and it was because he was not only human but was also fully divine (God).

The Mind of Mankind

> *"I, Daniel, was troubled in spirit, and the visions that passed through my mind disturbed me." Dan. 7:15*

> *"Do not conform any longer to the pattern of this world but be transformed by the renewing of your mind. Then you will be able to test and approve what God's will is—his good, pleasing, and perfect will." Rom. 12:2*

The plethora of thoughts that come to our minds have many potential sources. Differentiating between these sources takes wisdom, knowledge, and spiritual discernment. I would wager that most of us rarely consider the sources of the battles within our minds, but perhaps it is worth considering. One of the interesting aspects about the battle within the mind of man is its unavoidability in our human experience. However, how we deal with this battle varies greatly. The thought processes of our minds are continuous, whether we are aware of them or not. All of us have thoughts enter our mind that we continuously and automatically deal with. Some thoughts take on greater importance, so we may contemplate and ponder these more than others. These "deeper" thoughts often foster more of an internal dialogue where we become consciously aware of the conversations we are having within our own minds. The internal dialogue surrounding these weightier thoughts may be related to critical decisions we need to make. Furthermore, many of our thoughts are a complex combination between influences from the past, our personality, preferences, values, environmental stimuli, and life experiences. What we do with our thoughts may have little impact on anything except the immediate situation we find ourselves in, while others may alter the course of this life and potentially even our eternal life.

We have all seen the cartoons where an angel sits on one shoulder and the devil sits on the other shoulder of a character, each whispering or shouting contrary points of influence. This is a common theme because it is a common experience for us all. We cannot have a fully functioning mind without experiencing this. To be sure, these types of competing thoughts may be over things that have little moral or spiritual significance, but there are also competing thoughts that have tremendous influence over the path we walk and the reality we experience in this life. When it comes to good and evil, having a morality based on the words and actions of Jesus Christ can create a foundation that is in stark contrast to the words from the minds of men and the mind of Satan.

Sources of Input

The mind is the starting point for almost all the things that cause inward and outward motion in our lives. Most certainly the mind is influenced by many things, including our past, current situations, the words of others, the thoughts presented by the Holy Spirit, and perhaps more often than we would like, Satan's voice of influence. We simply cannot know the full extent of spiritual influences in the world, or in our lives. Yet, we can know that we were created with a capacity to engage with the spiritual world. If we can engage with the spiritual world, then the greater discernment we have about the nature of the forces within this world, the greater the chance we have of turning the battle of the mind into fruitful outcomes rather than creating a history of decisions and actions that perpetuate varying degrees of regret. Amidst this battle, I submit that if we are to win the battle for good, then we cannot do it without the direction of the Holy Spirit:

> *"For who among men knows the thoughts of a man except the man's spirit within him? In the same way no one knows the thoughts of God except the Spirit of God." 1 Cor. 2:11*

As we addressed in earlier chapters, we also need to evaluate if there is a distinct personality behind our thoughts, because deciphering good from evil is important in deciding how we respond to various things that come across our minds. There are certainly some thoughts that we need to immediately rebuke because of their nature. As the verse below supports, the natural state of man without the indwelling of the Holy Spirit is corrupt:

> *"They plot injustice and say, 'We have devised a perfect plan!' Surely the mind and heart of man are cunning."*
> *Ps. 64:6*

If you believe mankind is nothing more than another animal that inhabits the planet, then thoughts cannot be characterized as good or bad because you need a moral foundation to decide what is good or evil. A mere animal is not driven by a moral compass. If you are a believer in a moral God who created all things, then you have a potential foundation from which to hang your decisions of right and wrong. For much of western civilization the Bible has been the principal foundation for determining morality. Many hold the Bible to be the authority on truth and morality because it is believed to be the inspired Word of God by many who claim to be Christians. Unfortunately, many claim the religion of Christianity without being filled with the Holy Spirit and without a knowledge of the Scripture. Religion and a relationship with God are not the same thing. A relationship with Christ saves us, not religion:

> *"For the mind of the flesh is death; but the mind of the Spirit is life and peace: because the mind of the flesh is enmity against God; for it is not subject to the law of God, neither indeed can it be: and they that are in the flesh cannot please God." Rom. 8:6–8*

Whose Thought Was That?

If Satan attempted to sway Jesus's mind, how much more will he try to sway God's imperfect image bearers? Part of the assault of Satan's disinformation game is played out in our media today. If you observe the work of the media, you will likely conclude that a significant segment of it has a primary purpose to not present factual news, but rather to create fear and anxiety through nothing more than lies, speculation, and distortions.

The source of fear and anxiety is not and cannot be the Spirit of God. Rather, where irrational fears and anxiety exist, be aware that forces of evil are likely to be at work. Seriously, can we possibly watch the continuous deception in the mainstream media or Hollywood's motion picture industry without it influencing our mind's thoughts? The point is, it is a continual struggle to not allow our minds to be polluted by the world because the world is in our face continually. If we are not protecting our mind from this, then we will be influenced by it. Yes, we can shut down some of the thoughts that are being driven by the world around us, but the longer we entertain these thoughts, the more difficult it becomes to live beyond their influence. If we are not making the Word of God the primary influence in our lives, then we begin to look more and more like the world we live in:

> *"Religion that God our Father accepts as pure and faultless is this: to look after orphans and widows in their distress and to keep oneself from being polluted by the world." James 1:27*

> *"Jesus prayed: 'I have given them your word and the world has hated them, for they are not of the world any more than I am of the world. My prayer is not that you take them out of the world but that you protect them from the evil one.'" John 17: 14–15*

The Source of Life

Jesus came so that we might have life and have it more abundantly, but it is only through a continual relationship with him that we have hope of overcoming the negative influences of the world. To the best of our ability, we have to "take every thought captive" and evaluate that thought through the influence of the Holy Spirit to come up with right reactions to the bombardment of information our minds take in. Just because we are Christians does not mean we automatically have full control over our minds. Yet as believers we have a distinct advantage to discern what is good and what is evil because of the Spirit within us.

"The person with the Spirit makes judgments about all things, but such a person is not subject to merely human judgments, for, 'Who has known the mind of the Lord so as to instruct him?' But we have the mind of Christ." 1 Cor. 2:16

The Imagination

This is not a time for a full discussion on the topic of our imagination, but it is an intriguing subject. The truth is, we have been gifted with an imagination. God has the greatest imagination of all, which is visibly evident in all that he has created. Because we were made in his image we also have an imagination. The imagination has been woven into our fabric as his children, and as such, it can most certainly be stimulated by the Holy Spirit and create very positive outcomes. The imagination can also conjure up many playful and fun things in our lives. Yet regretfully, destructive thoughts can also be thrown into our imagination, as mentioned above. The imagination is like most gifts God has given us–it can be used for good purposes, or it can be distorted and used for evil:

"The weapons we fight with are not the weapons of the world. On the contrary, they have divine power to demolish strongholds. We demolish arguments and every pretension that sets itself up against the knowledge of God, and we take captive every thought to make it obedient to Christ." 2 Cor. 10:4–5

Life Story

As I was talking to a friend about adding personal stories to supplement this book, he said, "You need to add the bear story." The full bear story is far too long to add to this book, but let me summarize parts of it, as it relates to relinquishing elements of life into God's hands.

I enjoy the great outdoors in the Colorado mountains very much, and I have explored the mountain wilderness here over the past four decades. I am certain God has been a part of my hunting and wilderness experiences, just as he is with me on all journeys. Because God goes everywhere with me I am never without companionship. For example, I have had several overnight solo hunting trips in some pretty harsh winter weather conditions, but I always feel as though I am protected.

A few years back I was reluctantly changing elk hunting areas because in my previous area the elk herd had drastically diminished. I decided to go back to an area that I had hunted a decade prior, an area I left because the elk herd was never very abundant. It always felt like I was chasing six elk in a ten square mile area. Most of the time, that doesn't work out very well. To explore the prospects of hunting this area again, I took a late summer scouting expedition, and I directly asked God to give me a sign if the spot I was hiking into was where I was supposed hunt in a couple months. When I reached the specific meadow, I thought would provide the best opportunity for success, I found a dozen elk beds from the night before.

This was awesome! I felt like God was confirming that, "Yes, this is the place I should be." After observing the area for 30 minutes, I started walking the tree line around the West side of the meadow. When I was about ready to head back down the trail to my truck, I saw the biggest bear I have ever seen in Colorado emerge from the forest on the opposing side of this open area. I was hidden well enough, and he was not in a position to catch my scent, so from behind a fallen tree where he was unlikely to see me, I took a little time to attempt taking photos of him. It was getting close to dark, and I preferred walking out with some daylight, not to mention I did not want him to know I was there, so I departed fairly quickly to make my way back down the trail to my truck.

As I ventured away from the meadow, I felt like I was now faced with a bit of a test regarding whether I should hunt in this area or not. Do I trust God because he gave me the sign that I asked for, finding evidence of elk in the meadow? Or do I fearfully decide not to hunt in this large bear's home domain? Since I felt the bear was potentially a test of my faith, I elected to believe in God's sign of provision rather than be dominated by fear.

Two months later I was walking into this area an hour before daylight on opening day of elk hunting season. There was enough light from the stars and moon to allow me to hike in the dark without a flashlight. As I was hiking in, I was slowly catching up to three hunters ahead of me on the trail. They were using flashlights to light their path. Because I had no flashlight for them to see, and because their own flashlights hampered their vision of anything beyond the extent of their beams of light, they were unaware I was coming up behind them. I could have walked past them on the trail, as my pace was greater than theirs, but I was certain they were headed to the same meadow I intended to hunt. For me to walk past them and then hunt where they were likely to go would present a conflict of interest for all.

I was faced with a dilemma. When I plan a hunt, I typically take into account some degree of detail, and having these other hunters present was not part of the plan! There's an old hunting philosophy that goes, "Plan the hunt, and hunt the plan." It was my desire to hunt my plan that day. Yet while I walked behind the other hunters in the dark, I decided not to be competitive by trying to outpace them to the desired meadow. It is unlike me to easily yield, but at that moment I conversed with God saying, "You must have a better plan in mind, so I will go with whatever you have planned." Part of my growing philosophy and belief is that if my plans get changed that perhaps God is behind the change, and if so then he has something better in mind. At this moment I chose to rest in that belief, alter my direction, and trust in his presence.

To my family's relief, I hunt with a handheld GPS. It's too easy to get turned around and lost in the mountains, and the GPS allows me some security in going cross county rather than depending on trails. Thankfully, I had enough waypoints in my GPS that no matter where I went, I would be able to find my way back to my truck. I decided to yield to God's new plan for the day, I left the original trail and headed on an uncharted course. I walked through the moonlit forest and up the mountain until I found a ridge that traversed over and above the area I was originally going to hunt. The story will simply get too long if I were to express all that went on that day, but God was involved in the entire day. Most memorably, God allowed me to see my big bear's fresh tracks in the snow. The tracks indicated my bear friend had headed off in a direction away from where I would be gifted with a bull elk about an hour later.

It turned out that I downed a bull elk literally yards from where I saw the bear and took the photos of him at the end of my summer scouting trip. This happened after the morning hunters had left the area, discouraged because they had not seen any elk. Have you ever noticed that God tends to be rather poetic and creative when he shows evidence of his presence? Well, in this situation he made his goodness known by gifting me with an elk in the very spot where I saw the bear during the summer and engaged in conversations with him about hunting in the bears domain. Again, there were many elements to this day that I don't have time to share, but it was clearly a day filled with the Spirit's direction.

I truly feel like this was an orchestrated event that began when I asked God to show me a positive sign I should hunt this area, which he proceeded to give me. Then he immediately threw in the test of potentially becoming an unwelcome visitor in the large bear's domain. I chose to go with what I felt was God's positive answer to hunt in this meadow, but in the process I would have to deny the potential fear of walking into the bear's domain before daylight. When opening morning came, I was also confronted with creating unwanted competition with the other hunters for this prime hunting spot. I am rather certain that a primary element to the success of this experience was due to yielding my own will, in order to not infringe on the other hunters' plans.

In summary, this day required my faith to dominate my fear, and then it required a relinquishment of my plans and a belief that God might have something better in mind. Never did I believe making the change of plans limited my potential for a successful hunt; I just figured God had a better plan. In turn, these elements allowed me to experience a divinely orchestrated day. God's ways are always better, but we often must release our own willfulness to enjoy the benefits of his directed paths/plans. We also need to become as little children to see that God is walking, and even playing, with us throughout our lives.

Living Beyond Ourselves

Out of our own human strength, the struggle with sin is nearly impossible to conquer. We may find people and relationships that help steer us away from temptation, but the only true hope to rise above sin is through the indwelling of the Holy Spirit. The Spirit of God helps us live beyond ourselves, though given the world we live in, this is not an easy task. Just because the Spirit indwells us does not always mean we are inviting and allowing the Spirit to direct us. To allow the Spirit to work in us takes a continuous effort towards ongoing communication. A bedtime prayer is not enough communication for most of us to ward off the temptations of Satan, the influences of the world, and the battles in our minds.

Questions to Ponder

Was there a concept or statement in this chapter that struck you the most? Explain why.

What are some battles within your mind?

Do you feel you have control over the battle?

How do you control the battles that come to your mind?

CHAPTER 10

Broken by Sin

All Are Broken

WE ARE ALL BROKEN people who have our own personal bents toward sin. By this I mean that as unique as every human is, so are the specifics of our brokenness. Although our sin nature is universal, our tendencies for certain sins vary because we are all distinctively singular beings. The inner workings of our minds and the many behavioral and emotional triggers we have cause sins that are somewhat specific to each of us. Because of this, the nature of our repentance before God takes on a personal nature. God is a God of the masses, but he is also a God who is involved with us individually. We are his children, and like every good father he knows us and works with us one-on-one as he grows us with personalized care. Because of the internal dwelling of the Holy Spirit, those who walk with Jesus can come to experience this individualized relationship.

When referring to brokenness, I am referencing our sin nature and the control, or lack of control, we have over that sin nature. Two individuals can illustrate what I mean by this:

One is a pastor who has been a Christian striving to become more Christ-like since a very young age. Our view of such a person would generally be one of admiration due to the self-control and discipline that we see demonstrated in his or her life. The other person is someone who has newly come to Christ but he or she still drinks too much, is involved in recreational drugs, and has sex with multiple partners. Now, we might think the pastor is entitled to feel a sense of "arrival," as far as being pleasing to God due to his or her outward appearance of self-control, while the other person might feel a deep regret over his or her lifestyle and a failure to control it.

I submit that both people, if they are truly being transformed by God, each have internal struggles within their minds and their own set of spiritual victories and failures regarding sin:

> *"For all have sinned and fall short of the glory of God."*
> *Rom. 3:23*

Despite the great role models' pastors appear to be, they know their internal relationship with God is anything but static or completed. If active in their faith, both people in our example will be undergoing continual refinement by way of the Holy Spirit until the day they die. The Holy Spirit convicts each of them of the areas of which they need to gain control. Both have to release elements of their life over to Jesus in order to further their journey towards holiness, towards Christlikeness. The pastor may be working on controlling his/her tongue towards their beloved spouse or battling feelings of jealousy toward another person in ministry who appears to have gained more acknowledgments than they have. These internal struggles are not clearly seen on the outside, but there are nonetheless battles in a perpetual process of refinement.

The other man or woman may still be caught in their sinful lifestyle, but through the Holy Spirit, God is convicting them to eliminate drug use and to separate from some of the destructive friendships and activities in which they are currently involved. From a mainstream Christian view, this person may not be seen as "saved" and or "born again" because of his or her lifestyle. But, if both of these people have accepted Christ as their Lord and Savior, then the truth is God is at work in their lives and God cares deeply and uniquely for both of them:

> *"Jesus said, "For God so loved the world that he gave his one and only Son, that whoever believes in him shall not perish but have eternal life. For God did not send his Son*

> *into the world to condemn the world, but to save the world*
> *through him." John 3:16–17*

The fact is, God can use both of them for the purposes of His kingdom on earth. Each can be used by God in the settings where God places them by sharing their faith and expressing their personal struggles. The beauty and the difficulty in this process of transformation by the guidance of the Holy Spirit is its perpetual nature. It does not stop when we have overcome a particular sin. This ongoing process of refinement is called "sanctification," and it continues as long as we are in an abiding relationship with Jesus on this earth.

Work of Sanctification

This process of growth with God is a wonderful thing, but at times it can feel burdensome. Making decisions about how we are to live can be an ongoing battle of the mind and spirit. A walk with God in this life is like climbing hills—sometimes we get exhausted by a daunting stretch of steep hills that challenge our very being, and then God seems to give us a refreshing ledge to stand on for a period of time. There are moments when we feel confirmed for our efforts and we sense a peace about life, but then we are summoned to climb to the next level God has laid out before us. We learn to trust in God because of his past faithfulness, and we have an assurance that as we walk the path he sets before us, we will see good throughout the journey with him:

> *"And we know that in all things God works for the good of*
> *those who love him, who have been called according to his*
> *purpose." Rom. 8:28*

God is not pushy, but he is persistent. So when we fall, he stands us back up again and gives us new opportunities to move forward. As we live in this world and walk with God, we will always be faced with the next stretch of hill, which is the next opportunity to become stronger and more useful to others as we progress through this life. We will never reach the final plateau because it is not possible for us to perfectly embody God's level of holiness as Jesus did. What matters to God is the "heart" we put into the climb as well as our attentiveness to his voice and our willingness to adapt to his will. I believe that God doesn't need to break our will through trials if our hearts are attentive to his promptings, although some trials are allowed in our lives to grow us into what he would like us to be. He is a gracious father, and when we have given our lives to him, he will prompt us and, if necessary, bend us to conform more to the image of his son Jesus:

> *"Therefore, since we are surrounded by such a great cloud of witnesses, let us throw off everything that hinders and the sin that so easily entangles, and let us run with perseverance the race marked out for us." Heb. 12:1*

Overcoming

God certainly does not intend for this journey to be a burden. God refines us on this trek and his Holy Spirit guides our hearts in the process, but God also intends for us to have joy in our lives. He does not want us to beat ourselves up over the things we are not, or the things we think he wants us to become. When we mess up on this journey, we can find relief through acknowledging our sin and asking for forgiveness. If we do not feel strong enough for parts of the journey, we can ask God to give us strength or even to carry us for a time. God loves us and he wants us to have peace. Beating ourselves up only weakens us and makes climbing to the next level self-defeating and improbable. Satan also loves to talk down about us through our thought life, reminding us of our failures and making us feel unworthy. He does this to further separate us from God—to hold us back from the freedom found in releasing our failures to the profound healing that awaits us through our repentance, which is then followed by God's cleansing forgiveness. Satan wants us to abandon our walk with God through creating guilt, feelings of unworthiness, and a lack of hope. The good news is, Jesus calls us brothers and sisters, and

God wants to adopt us as children with full access to the Father/ King, through the indwelling of his Holy Spirit.

S.I.N. = Separation in Nature

Sin is not an easy topic to address primarily because the word brings so many different connotations to mind. At least in the United States where I live, the predominant understanding of the word *sin* comes from a Judeo-Christian foundation. Although the majority of Americans have little understanding of the Bible, most understand there is something called sin. Most humans generally seem to understand that there are both good and bad behaviors. Unfortunately, as our society moves further away from the authority of Scripture, the less likely people are to believe in such a thing as sin because they lack the foundational understanding about the character of good versus evil. Without a standard for morality, many people operate on an unstable foundation of moral relativism, which basically means that each person decides for him or herself what is right and wrong. Fortunately, there seem to be certain foundational truths about good and evil that are written on the heart of mankind; otherwise our world would be in a far worse state than it is already:

> *"The LORD saw how great man's wickedness on the earth*
> *had become, and that every inclination of the thoughts of*
> *his heart was only evil all the time." Gen. 6:5*

Sin interferes with a favorable standing before our Holy God because at its very core, sin causes relational separation from God. Like oil separates from water so sin separates us from God. Therefore, our sin can negatively interfere in our relationship with God. The great news is, Jesus created a path of forgiveness. Through Christ's sacrifice and our willful repentance, we can remain in communion with God:

> *"Therefore, my brothers, I want you to know that through*
> *Jesus the forgiveness of sins is proclaimed to you." Acts 13:38*

*"Therefore, there is now no condemnation for those who
are in Christ Jesus, because through Christ Jesus the law of
the Spirit of life set me free from the law of sin and death."
Rom. 8:1*

Sin's Perpetual Nature

A few years back, I was speaking with a pastor of an inner-city
church about sin and temptation. As we compared notes about
temptations that are more prevalent among the poor versus the
upper class, he mentioned the saying, "different devils for different levels." It is an interesting observation that temptations and
sin tendencies certainly vary depending on the cultures, com-
munities, and families where we reside. Due to our fallen human
nature, there is no doubt that temptation/tendencies towards sin
are present in all of us. It is also evident that sin can engulf a life
so aggressively that the chance for redemption seems remote. The
question is whether the level and degree of sin are merely a chance
issue or if there could be entrenched spiritual forces at work. As we
addressed earlier, there are those who believe demonic influences
stay within certain tribes and families. The idea is that demonic
spirits embed themselves in a family unit and thus the sons and/
or daughters end up with the same influences from demonic spirits who continue to follow, pursue, and tempt them with the sins
which their immediate family and past ancestors were tempted
by. A term for this family-oriented form of demonic influence
is familiar spirits. Thus, familiar spirits are familiar with a given
family—they know the family weaknesses and have become effective at causing the family to carry the curse of a particular sin from
generation to generation. This concept stems from several similar
Old Testament passages. Here is one:

> *"The LORD is slow to anger, abounding in love and forgiv-
> ing sin and rebellion. Yet he does not leave the guilty un-
> punished; he punishes the children for the sin of the fathers
> to the third and fourth generation." Num. 14:18*

Modern psychology expresses that such things as sexual abuse, alcoholism, anger issues, etc. can develop through modeling and perhaps through some genetic influence. This view may certainly be valid in certain situations, but it leaves out the realm of spiritual influences within family systems. The Old Testament makes clear that blessings and curses may be passed on to the third and fourth generations. Could it be that without God's hand of protection over a family, Satan may be given a foothold that is passed on generationally? This is not an easy subject because there are those, including Christians, who completely ignore the potential reality of demonic influence.

Let's revisit the phrase, "different devils for different levels" for a moment. My pastor-friend believes the materially poor better understand their sin and their helplessness and are therefore more likely to confess their sin and come and receive the forgiveness that Christ offers. On the other hand, typically the more affluent people of the world pridefully reject the idea they need a Savior because money has become their false foundation. This is certainly part of the reason Jesus said these words to his disciples:

> *"Again, I tell you, it is easier for a camel to go through the eye of a needle than for a rich man to enter the kingdom of God." Matt 19:24*

The Struggle with Sin

Paul's writings are filled with Spiritual truths that don't come from his natural, human mind but from a mind renewed by the Spirit. Yet despite this, even he admits his own struggle to contain his sin:

> *"For I know that good itself does not dwell in me, that is, in my sinful nature. For I have the desire to do what is good, but I cannot carry it out. For I do not do the good I want to do, but the evil I do not want to do—this I keep on doing. Now if I do what I do not want to do, it is no longer I who do it, but it is sin living in me that does it." Romans 7:18–20*

There is a spiritual war being fought. This battle is for the minds and the hearts of humankind. It begins in the mind, and once an idea or behavior sets up residence in our lives, it can be difficult to overcome. Once an idea or behavior moves from the mind to the heart, it then overflows by way of our speech and our actions/behaviors. Both positive and negative strongholds are created within us through repetition of either good or evil speech, actions, and assorted behaviors. Ultimately, behavioral habits and sin tendencies are formed through what first takes root in our minds:

> *"When tempted, no one should say, 'God is tempting me.' For God cannot be tempted by evil, nor does he tempt anyone; but each one is tempted when, by his own evil desire, he is dragged away and enticed. Then, after desire has conceived, it gives birth to sin; and sin, when it is full-grown, gives birth to death." James 1:13–15*

Justification

Adam and Eve were the crowning jewels of God's creation, as are all humans because we are his image bearers. Yet, Adam and Eve sinned against God even in their unbroken relational standing with God, or unfallen state. If they sinned in an unfallen state, then how will we in our *fallen* state have any chance of leading a fully virtuous life? God knows we are incapable of living a sinless life like Jesus did. Yet through Christ's death and by God's grace we are offered a path of forgiveness. It is through a relationship with Jesus in combination with repentance and forgiveness that grants us justification. Justification is for all times, present and future, and keeps the door to heaven open for those who follow Jesus, the savior of humanity. But since we are human we will continue to sin, even as we strive to become more Christ-like. The *good news* is, from Christ's death to the present, we live under a new covenant, and we receive forgiveness of our sins by means of repentance. Reflect on this repentant prayer of King David after he committed adultery with Bathsheba:

> *Have mercy on me, O God, according to your unfailing love; according to your great compassion blot out my transgressions.*
>
> *Wash away all my iniquity and cleanse me from my sin.*
>
> *For I know my transgressions,*
> *and my sin is always before me.*
>
> *Against you, you only, have I sinned and done what is evil in your sight, so that you are proved right when you speak and justified when you judge.*
>
> *Surely I was sinful at birth, sinful from the time my mother conceived me.*
>
> *Surely you desire truth in the inner parts; you teach me wisdom in the inmost place.*
>
> *Psa. 51:1–6*

May we come to God in a similar fashion.

Despite the Apostle Paul's accomplishments through the power of the Holy Spirit that was alive within in him, he had these words for us:

> *"Not that I have already obtained all this, or have already been made perfect, but I press on to take hold of that for which Christ Jesus took hold of me. Brothers, I do not consider myself yet to have taken hold of it. But one thing I do: Forgetting what is behind and straining toward what is ahead, I press on toward the goal to win the prize for which God has called me heavenward in Christ Jesus."*
> *Phil. 3:12–14*

None of us will arrive at a sinless life, but God does see our hearts and thus knows our desires. All our thoughts and actions are visible to God, and like a good Father he desires the best for us. The best for us is living in an ongoing, Spirit-filled, relationship with him. This communion is kept intact when we become his adopted children through a relationship with his son Jesus. And it is through a process of repentance and forgiveness that we are considered cleansed from our unrighteous state and worthy of being called Kids of the King.

Where Is Our Security

If we place our faith in the fleeting things of this world, then most of these things will fail us and hope will seem lost. However, if our hope is in Christ and his abiding presence along with the promise of the eternal Kingdom to come, then our perspective of hope drastically changes. The Bible makes it very clear that seeking after things in this world is like chasing after the wind, but when we place our faith and hope in things that have eternal significance, we will not be disappointed.

Each of us needs to honestly evaluate where our hope is placed. If we place our hope in our fellow man, our money, our elected officials, our health, or other elements of this world, then our hope will at some point be lost because everything in this life will ultimately fail us. The bottom line is, if there is anything we hold onto in this life, it will eventually be stripped from us, either while we are here or in our parting. How many times can we place our faith and our hope in things that are not of God and still retain a sense of hope? For hope to persevere against the odds, it needs to be placed in God alone, for he holds our past, our present, and our future in view. He has invited us to enjoy life with the Father, Son, and the Holy Spirit forever. With this promise in view, our focus should continually be realigned from earthly perspectives to eternal ones.

Do we hope more for someone's mortal life to be saved, or do we hope most for someone's eternal life to be secured? Do we hope for daily pleasure, or do we seek to be pleasing to God? Do we hope for monetary success so that we might possess more and more things, or do we use our monetary blessings to generously provide for the needs of others? The Bible states that we are aliens in this current, broken world because our true home is in with God in heaven. Do we live as if this world is our home or do we live with the confidence that our true home is yet to come? In the meantime, do we generously distribute our Father's love, care, kindness, enthusiasm, generosity, faith, and hope to his creation? We can't live for self and live for God.

Questions to Ponder

Was there on concept or statement in this chapter that struck you the most? Explain why.

If all sin separates us from God, is one sin greater than another?

Why do you think there is a persistent nature behind certain sins in your life?

What do you think causes you to go back to the same sin tendencies?

Concluding Thoughts

G OD WANTS US TO maintain a healthy fascination about the spiritual aspects of the world around us, yet he does not want it to be a burden or a source of fear. God desires us to have genuine, relational assurance in Him. Our deep faith will foster gratitude and hope in all things because of the confidence we have in him:

> "God has said, 'Never will I leave you; never will I forsake you.'" Hebrews 13:5

The amount of influence God has in our lives is most likely related to the amount of communication we choose to have with him. In one way or another, I believe this book is all about relationship. It is first and foremost about our relationship with the Triune God. Faith-filled followers of Jesus Christ are promised adoption into the family of God. Through this relationship with God, we are granted certain family privileges as kids of the King. Certainly, one of these privileges is the freedom of knowing God is at work, making the most of our lives even amid trials. We are not to be burden-carriers but freedom-proclaimers and recipients of God's peace through the indwelling of the Holy Spirit. Yes, there are other spiritual and earthly forces that want to steal our joy and diminish our freedom, but those forces cannot overcome the relational promises God makes to his children:

> *"For you did not receive a spirit that makes you a slave again to fear, but you received the Spirit of sonship. And by him we cry, 'Abba (Daddy), Father.'" Rom. 8:15*

I hope what you have read has opened your heart and your mind to ideas and realities you may not have considered before. It is my prayer that the Spirit of truth gives each reader discernment, picking up what is in alignment with God's perspective of reality and leaving behind anything that is not. Overall, I pray you have found the thoughts within inspiring, challenging, and intriguing. If you think any of the book could be beneficial to share with others, please do!

May you experience the peace, hope, freedom, and joy of being a Kid of the one, true King.

Peace,

Doc B

www.ingramcontent.com/pod-product-compliance
Lightning Source LLC
Chambersburg PA
CBHW070739030726
47601CB00001B/75